Nourishing Friendships

How to Make Friends You Love in Midlife and Beyond

Alisoun Mackenzie

Dedicated to my parents, Joe and Rosemary Wake, who inspired me to write this book. I'm so grateful to you both.

Contents

Introduction

Want more friends to speak to, go out with, and have fun with?

My intention in writing this book is to inspire and equip you with ways to do this, so you find it easier to make friends who value and cherish your friendship as much as you do.

You will soon have more friends

While it can feel lonely when you have few friends, you're not alone. Up to 22% of people don't have close friends. That means there are plenty of people out there waiting to meet you.

The other good news is that by making a few simple changes, you will be able to make friends with more confidence and ease.

But not just any friend. Rather, I encourage you to focus on nurturing nourishing friendships. Relationships with people who will bring out the best in you, love you, and support you, as much as you do them. This involves being intentional in selecting, making, and tending to friendships. It also means being spontaneous and open to the most unlikely friendships too.

Who is this book for?

This book is for you if you want more friends, and particularly if:

- You are lonely and yearn for the company of others.
- You're unsure how to make friends and want some tips.
- You're entering a new stage of life and want to connect with like-minded people for company, support, and fun.
- You'd like more local friends to talk to, go out with, and so you can support one another.
- You've grown apart from friends you've had in the past and want to make friends with people who 'get' who you are now.
- You're envious of people who have a close-knit group of friends and want to find your tribe.
- You want friends to do particular activities with.
- You want to cope better with friendship challenges and enjoy easier, more harmonious relationships.

I've written this book primarily for women in midlife and beyond, purely because this is who I support through my coaching practice and most of the stories I share are from people in this segment of the population.

That said, the approach I share to friendship is universal – whatever your age, gender, or life experience. It doesn't matter whether you're a young adult or in your wisdom years; single or in a relationship; a parent or childless; employed or unemployed; in business or retired; introvert or extrovert; able bodied or with physical impairments; neurodiverse or neurotypical. This book will help you to make and enjoy more friendships.

New friendship opportunities

Imagine looking back upon a life of nourishing friendships, fulfilling experiences, and cherished memories. All of this is within your reach.

Exactly what you take away from reading this book will depend on your unique circumstances.

I hope to make it easier for you to:

- Look forward to a future made better by good friends and life-enriching experiences that bring joy to your heart.

- Make, nurture, and keep good friends for as long as it feels good for them to be in your life.

- Enjoy friendships you can trust and rely upon – so you feel fully supported and cope better when things get tough.

- Feel a deeper sense of connection, belonging, and meaning through being part of a good group of friends who bring out the best in each other.

Friendship: my dad's final gift to me

We've all had different experiences that shape the relationships we have now. Like many, I've not always found it easy to make friends.

A couple of days after my dad died, I realised one of his greatest gifts.

I was sitting in tears on my sofa in the living room, looking out at a crisp December day. With a heavy sadness in my chest, I felt my world had stopped. Yet palm trees blowing about in the wind and my cats playing in the garden reminded me that life goes on. I was utterly exhausted from the shock and trauma of spending the last couple of weeks at Dad's bedside. Our last conversations still played a continual loop in my mind.

One thing I appreciated from that time was the constant stream of lovely messages from his friends who lived all around the world. Many shared the ways he'd enriched their lives and how much they valued his friendship.

His friends were people of all ages, many of whom he'd known for decades. He regularly called, visited, and talked about them, so we knew of most of them as a family. He had friends from university, Scottish country dancing, stamp collecting, travelling, working abroad for many years, and spending much of this time in Germany, where his wife lives. Despite health challenges latterly, he'd still prioritised his friends.

As I took another sip of my tea, I realised he'd been a major influence on the friends I have in my life, too. I don't remember him ever sitting me down or giving me friendship tips, though. It's more likely that I simply observed what he did at an unconscious level as a child and copied him.

While I found it hard to make friends as a child, I too now have a diverse range of friends from all around the world, many of whom have lasted over thirty years. Alongside family and health, they are one of the most important things in my life.

In that moment of awakening, I felt a new connection with my dad that transcends this physical realm. The heaviness in my heart lessened as I basked in gratitude for his gift.

I find friendships easier with age

As a young child, my friends were the other kids who lived in our street or classmates. I loved being able to run around and have fun with whoever was available. I didn't have a best friend but think I was relatively happy.

However, things changed when I was nine and moved to a new school where it was difficult to fit into a class where friendship groups had already formed. I was bullied and often felt like the odd one out. Thankfully, by my second year, I'd made some good friends and finally felt accepted when the other pupils voted me class captain.

But things took a turn for the worse when I went to high school, where I was bullied simply because I'd spent a couple of years at a private school. Yes, I had a few close friends in my form class, but as we spent more time in mixed classes, I found it increasingly harder. I hated high school and instead I found solace with friends I made through ice skating where I was judged less. It was a relief to spend time with people who cared more about our shared passion than which school I'd been to.

I carried my insecurities and emotional trauma of being bullied at school with me into my early twenties. And although I had a handful of close friends from school and work, I often felt a lack of connection with others.

I thought something was wrong with me – until I realised I simply hadn't found my tribe yet. How could I, when I'd lost sight of who I was? I didn't realise who I had the potential to become until I spent a year backpacking around the world. It was only then that friendships became easier, as I reconnected to who I was inside and spent more time with like-minded people. I came back from that year away with so much more confidence than the shy, lost young woman I'd been when I set off. Since then, I've found it much easier.

We are all human

That's not to say I'm perfect by any means. Like everyone else, I'm human with strengths and weaknesses, and I make mistakes. But I've learned that when upsets or misunderstandings are addressed with love and care, you can strengthen bonds, if both parties want to. I've also experienced the pain of losing friends who chose to end our friendship without any explanation.

The one thing that helps me cope with life is knowing that great experiences and memories with friends outweigh any downsides. I also believe we all do the best we can, with the skills and resources we have available to us in any moment. This makes it easier to accept and forgive myself and others when things go wrong.

What's your friendship story?

Your life experiences as a child often shape your adult friendships. Be mindful of your friendship story as you read through this book.

- What experiences did you have with friends when you were younger – good and bad?
- How did your early years shape your friendships in adult life?
- Have you ever had challenging times with friends?
- What's your friendship story – what you tell yourself about friendships, e.g. they are hard or easy, do friends hurt you or enrich your life?
- How have your early friendships shaped how you approach friendships now?

Welcome to this accidental book

While delivering one of my courses on how to live a joyful meaningful life, I invited the participants to ask friends for three words to describe them. Most of the women in the group said they didn't have friends to approach, which was a surprise and deeply saddened me.

Over the next year, those women regularly asked me to run a course to help them make friends. Having been surrounded by fabulous friends for the last few decades, and with over twenty years of experience as a life coach, communications trainer, and well-being specialist, I knew this was something I could do.

Around the same time, I also noticed that posts on social media asking for help to make friends often attracted lots of comments. So, I ran free online masterclasses and was surprised by the demand for these. Around the same time, the Covid pandemic had brought to the fore the vast number of people struggling with loneliness.

This all prompted me to release an online coaching programme called Nourishing Friends. And the results people quickly got from this blew me away. When I reconnected with some of the course participants a couple of years later, they still raved about how what they'd learned had made a huge impact on their friends and lives.

I intended to continue running these courses, but unfortunately, I fell ill with chronic fatigue and lacked the energy to do so. Some people who had attended my free events reached out for help but didn't have the money to invest in the course or coaching. So, turning the course into this book appeared an ideal way to support and impact more people.

Thanks to everyone who influenced this book

I like how books make learning more accessible, but before I decided to publish this book, I felt I needed to test my ideas with more people in their midlife years. So, I created a survey which was completed by over 130 women, from their 20s to 80s, and I spoke to women I thought would have valuable input.

I also received feedback from women as young as 17 saying they'd be interested in this book too. Interestingly, despite making my survey publicly available to all genders, no men completed it.

This book reflects the most common friendship challenges my clients and survey respondents said they face, the tips and ideas they shared, and topics they asked to know more about.

Thanks also to my mum and Christine McPherson for your invaluable insights when editing this book, and to all my friends who endured conversations about friendship. You have all helped me to write a better book than I would have done alone.

How to get the most from this book

This book has been written to be read from start to finish, as the content builds upon the previous chapter. Or you can dip in and out to check out topics of most interest to you.

Part 1: Friendship Foundations – discover empowering friendship secrets, the evolution of friendships as we age, and tips for being and choosing good friends.

Part 2: Seven Steps to Nourishing Friendships – simple steps to enjoy more good times with friends for years to come. Follow these so you find it easier to make friends with people who will enrich your life.

Part 3: Skills to Transform Your Friendships – tips and practical skills are woven all through this book. In this final section, I've expanded upon skills people most frequently asked about during my research .

Supporting this book

- **Nourishing Friendships Workbook** – creating change involves taking action and embracing new habits. This accompanying workbook includes practical exercises and plenty of blank journal pages to capture all your thoughts and ideas, so you find it easier to enjoy more good friendships. Check it out on Amazon or via my website – www.alisoun.com/books

- **Nourishing Friends Notebook** – designed to make it easier for you to keep on top of new friendships and remember important information about your friends. Available on Amazon or via my website – www.alisoun.com/books

- **Friendship Resources** – you will also find other resources and support services available to help you on your friendship journey on my website. These include blogs, videos, training courses, and online coaching. Check these out on my website – alisoun.com/friends

Your invitation to enjoy fabulous nourishing friends

Whatever your experiences with friends to date, those who will benefit the most from what I share here are people who commit to investing in themselves and taking action. By setting aside time to read this book and working through the practical exercises, you'll be well on your way to more friendships soon.

We also bring our thoughts and dreams alive when we discuss them with others. So I encourage you to share your thoughts and insights with people you know, in groups you're part of or run, at classes, workshops, or book clubs, or with me on social media.

Most importantly, enjoy the adventure of making fabulous new nourishing friends.

With love and gratitude,

Alisoun x

Part One
Friendship Foundations

Nourishing Friendships Workbook
Some chapters include practical exercises that I've consolidated into a
Nourishing Friendships Workbook. This is available as a paperback on
Amazon or through my website: alisoun.com/friends

Chapter 1
Common Reasons Adults Have Few Friends

Having few friends is more common than you think

When you have few friends, it can feel like everyone else is out having fun with theirs. But that's often not the case.

Research consistently shows that too many people feel lonely and wish they had more friends. A study published in December 2021 found that 7% of Britons say they don't have any close friends, increasing to 9% for people over the age of 40[1]. This increases again to 10% of people who describe themselves as introverts. Figures in the US are similar, with some surveys finding that up to 22% of people have no friends. The good news is, though, this means there are plenty of people out there who are ready and keen to become one of your friends.

But how do you connect with them? This book will show you how, although the best way forward for you also partly depends on why you currently have few friends. It's only when you understand this that you can decide what to change about how you approach future friendships.

---

1. https://yougov.co.uk/society/articles/38493-yougov-friendship-study-part-1-close-friends-and-b

You might not have control over all the factors contributing to your current situation. For instance, childhood neglect, or abuse or trauma at any age can significantly impact the quality of all your adult relationships, unless you have completely healed from them. However, no matter what your experience of life to date, there will be things you can do differently so that you find it easier to make and keep good friends in the future.

As you read through this chapter, notice which reasons are true for you – both those you can do something about, and limitations beyond your control. The intention of doing this is not to assign any blame or criticism, but rather to highlight reasons as explanations for the past – you can choose whether to let go of these issues or take with you into the future. This chapter is also intended to give you a greater perspective on challenges which others face.

1. Not making time for friends in your life

People with plenty of friends prioritise their friendships. They spend time with existing friends and take the initiative to make and nurture new ones. And while time can be scarce, many busy people are still surrounded by good friends.

Of course, there are times when you may have to temporarily step back from friends, e.g. if you're ill, caring for someone, or facing a challenging situation that you need to deal with. But always remember to re-engage when these things ease.

Ultimately, your mindset, how you cope with life, and make time for friends, determines the friends and type of friendships you have.

2. Not meeting enough like-minded people

When we are young, many of our friends are born from the people in our daily lives, e.g. at school, work, or locally. However, as we get older, friendships grow less organically, and we need to be more intentional about meeting and nurturing relationships with like-minded people – especially during times of change. While this might initially take more effort, it also gives you the opportunity to be more selective over who you spend time with, and in doing so you can develop more deeper, meaningful friendships. That's what I encourage you to do in this book.

~

I used to think there was something wrong with me because I didn't feel I fitted in at school or the corporate world – until I realised I was simply in the wrong environments where there weren't many like-minded people. I hadn't found my tribe. That's why over the years I've set up and run groups, e.g. a travel club and business networking groups. This made it easier to attract and meet plenty of lovely people who have become good friends.

~

You don't need to set up your own new group, though. Joining clubs and classes where you'll meet like-minded people, or people at a similar stage of life, is a great step in the right direction, and it will also boost your mental health and social life. An internet search for local friendship groups or clubs for older people, yields lots of results and options.

3. Waiting for people to invite you out

One of the most common reasons people let friends slip through their fingers is that they don't invite enough people out. This could be due to a fear of rejection, not feeling good enough, or just simply a lack of confidence.

Yet, inviting people you've met to go out for a chat or to join you on an activity makes all the difference. Likewise, consider doing the same with friends you liked but have lost touch with. Ask lots of people and expect some to say 'no'. But don't give up. You only need a few people to say 'yes' and the more people you ask out, the more friends you're likely to make.

4. Friends moving on

As we go through life it's natural to lose friends, as some move away, change jobs, transition to another stage of life, or, sadly, die. Common examples include when your friends get married, have children when you don't, become carers, travel a lot, become grandparents, or retire. Of course, it could be you who moves on. And all this is natural. Most people we meet are only in our lives for a limited time. Lifelong friends are the exception. That's why it's important to continue to meet new people and nurture existing relationships.

5. Parenthood

Quite rightly, becoming a parent changes your priorities in life, but it also impacts friendships. First-time parents often make new friends with others in the same situation, while spending less time with child-free people and those with more spare time in their life. Not surprisingly many new close friendships are often forged during this time, when children are young. However, it's common for many of these friendships to drift apart when children grow up and parents finally have the freedom to do what they want to do – often finding their interests differ to those of their friends who were part of their young parent journey. As their life changes and they want to spend time with like-minded people, sometimes they reconnect with friends they had before their children were born.

'Being a teenage single parent I was either working hard or sleeping while everyone else was out having fun. I am naturally a social person but didn't have much time or energy for friends. I was too exhausted. Now over twenty years later, I feel like I'm starting again.' Lucy

6. Being childless

With almost 20% of women in the UK reaching menopause without children – many not through choice – there are a huge number of people who lose friends through not having children.

Parents become part of a club that childless people are excluded from forever. Everyone I've spoken to who is involuntarily childless has similar stories. Most can also recount times when people have judged them, put them down, or told them they are selfish because they don't have children – shockingly most often from mums. I experienced this myself, and that's why I made such a conscious effort to make friends with other childless people. If I hadn't done this, I'm sure I would have endured many lonely years.

∾

'I have lots of good friends I've known for many years, and I love them dearly. But they are all mothers, and as I'm sad that I'm childless I can feel very isolated when they talk about their children all the time. I find it easier to spend time with male friends who are less children focussed.' Sally

∾

7. Divorce or relationship breakdown

It's natural to lose some friends when relationships break down, particularly if mutual friends have a closer relationship with one person.

I remember when I was getting divorced, the one thing I worried about most was losing friends. It took effort on my part to continue to nurture friendships with those I was closest to and wanted to stay in touch with. Almost twenty years later, it's wonderful that some of my closest friends are still those I met through my first marriage.

This, however, isn't everyone's experience. Some people have told me they lost mutual friends, while others said their friendships improved after a break-up as they had more time for friends. If you're going through a break-up, decide which friendships, if any, you want to keep and make time to continue to nurture them.

8. Changing jobs and working from home

Changing jobs can often lead to the loss of friends and leave you feeling isolated if you have relied upon colleagues for company and social contact – unless you make an effort to stay in touch with those you were closest to. But changing jobs can also be an opportunity to connect with people who are more aligned with who you are.

Since the Covid-19 pandemic, more people are socially isolated and missing out on friendships because they're working from home. It will be interesting to see how this unfolds over the long-term and how society and the social beings we are will adapt to this new norm.

9. Retiring

Likewise, your experience of friendships in retirement depends on the extent you invested in friendships while you were working, as well as whether your existing friends have retired or are working. It's easier if you have other friends who have also retired. However, many people reach retirement with time to fill and a need to meet new people.

Everything I share in this book will help you to do this. You'll also find tips and insights about friendships in retirement in Chapters 5 and 24, the latter all being from people who have retired.

10. Being a caregiver

While caring for a loved one may be something you want or need to do, one impact can be less time for friendships. This can feel overwhelming, lonely, isolating, and draining – especially if it's all-consuming over a long period, your time is often spent at hospital or medical appointments, or you're a sandwich generation caregiver (caring for parents, children, and/or grandchildren all at the same time). In such situations, arranging breaks and spending time with friends is particularly important to preserve your own wellbeing. Consider respite care, setting up a support network, or using caregiving apps to help organise care, monitor medication, and keep an eye on loved ones remotely.

～

'Some of the best advice I got from a friend was to pay people to come in and keep my husband company so I could get a break and go out with friends. Being a carer is exhausting and lonely. Going out with friends

gives you the chance to remember who you are: to have fun, enjoy yourself, and feel supported. The person you care for may not like you going out, but to be the best support to them, you need to look after yourself too.'
Gillian

∿

11. Moving to a new place

Moving house is one of the most obvious reasons for not having many local friends – unless you've moved somewhere you already know people.

In a new place it can sometimes feel like everyone is too busy or already in established friendship groups that are hard to break into. That's why seeking out other newcomers initially could be an easier way to build friendships. Some places even have groups set up specifically to welcome people to the area. Or you can join organised clubs, groups, or local activities to meet like-minded people. You could check out local groups on Facebook, MeetUp.com, or notice boards at your local supermarket or library to see what's available.

If you or a friend moves away, making an effort to stay in touch during the first year apart can have a significant impact on the sustainability of your friendship. Thankfully, social media and Zoom have made it easier to stay in touch with friends living a distance away.

12. Illness

Life-threatening and long-term chronic illnesses (physical, mental, and emotional) and physical limitations can hugely limit our ability to meet people and maintain friendships – whatever your age. It can, however, also be a time when good friends can provide critical emotional and physical support.

∿

I feel so grateful to have had lots of good friends, locally and online, before I became ill with chronic fatigue. For the last few years I've not had the energy to see anyone other than my closest friends who have been invaluable in helping me cope better and recover.

~

Thankfully there are many ways to participate in online activities, connect with people, and socialise from home. I'm not saying it's easy; often it's not, particularly if you've been unwell for a long time. However, I've spoken to quite a few people who have said that being able to talk to friends or have Zoom calls, helps ease their isolation and loneliness.

13. A lack of appreciation for neurodiversity

This huge topic often causes misunderstandings, upsets, exclusion, and social isolation for those who are wired differently – simply because they think, learn, and act differently to what is considered the norm. Yet, this represents around 15-20% of the population[2] and it seems more and more people are being 'tested' or diagnosed, so the norm seems to be becoming less so. Neuro-differences include Autism Spectrum Disorder (ASD, including what was formerly known as Aspergers), Attention Deficit Hyperactivity Disorder (ADHD), Dyslexia, Dyspraxia, Tourette's, and social anxiety.

~

'ADHD means that it's hard for me to maintain friendships. I know I don't reach out or catch up as much as some of my friends would like, but that doesn't mean I don't care. I just get distracted. I love it when they get in touch and enjoy seeing them. But I also seem to need my own space more than they do.' Toni

~

If you are neurodiverse (or think you could be) I encourage you to focus on your natural talents as you read this book, consider how your

---

2. https://www.neurodiversityweek.com/introduction

behaviours impact friendships, and what you could do to make friendships easier. For example, discuss your needs and natural traits with friends so they can be a better friend to you. If you're neurotypical (your brain works in the way society expects), I encourage you to value and appreciate all the good qualities of neurodiverse friends and to seek to understand their perspective better. We are all unique with something valuable to offer to friendship.

14. Friends die

While the only certainty in life is death, when you lose a close friend, it's common to feel a deep sense of loss – especially if you shared a deep emotional connection, were in touch regularly, or provided practical support to one another. It can be devastating.

∾

I'll always remember my gran at just under ninety, telling me she was ready to go. As someone who loved her dearly, I told her I didn't want her to die. But she told me, 'Darling, your grandfather and most of my friends are no longer here. I don't have anyone left to talk to and reminisce about my younger days and the good times I've had in life.' While I didn't like what I heard, I realised I hadn't thought about things from my gran's perspective. I also learned another important message: to keep making friends all through life, including with people younger than me.

∾

15. Lack of interests or hobbies

Hobbies and shared interests are some of the best ways to meet people who enjoy the same activities as you, and there are groups for almost every hobby and interest you can think of. If you don't have many interests, consider what you'd like to try, then research local or online groups. If you can't find a group for your activity of choice, you could set one up yourself. This is something I've done several times to meet like-minded people.

16. Your behaviours

Our ability to get on with people and make friends depends upon our personality traits, the way we're wired, and our behaviours. Most of us learn to adapt our behaviours to 'fit in' with the environments where we spend time. But this isn't always easy as everyone has different communication styles, e.g. introvert or extrovert, direct versus chatty, quiet versus loud, or people-focussed versus task-focussed.

When you normally display socially acceptable behaviours to the environments you're in, people are more likely to tolerate when you act out of character. However, if you consistently express extreme negative behaviours, you're likely to find it harder to make and keep friends. Sometimes being positive can cost you friendships, too, particularly with people who are struggling and are consumed in what's wrong with their own life. So be mindful of how all your behaviours impact friendships.

If you generally find relationships hard, consider how your behaviours could be costing you friends, e.g. if you could come across as being a bully, needy, overly critical, negative, bitchy, argumentative, unreliable, aggressive, judgemental, abusive, or slow to respond. Likewise, if you regularly feel hurt, upset, rejected, jealous, disappointed, or not good enough, do you have unmet needs or emotional trauma that you're projecting onto friendships?

Unresolved traumas can negatively impact friendships in many ways, such as causing trust issues; doubts, fears, and anxieties; a reluctance to form close bonds or, conversely, an excessive dependence on others; emotional volatility; deep anger, hopelessness, shame, or sadness; social anxiety or withdrawal; overly rigid boundaries that push people away, or weak, harmful boundaries.

I encourage you to reflect on how your behaviours impact your friendships, and to be compassionate – yet firm where necessary – with people who don't treat you well. There's usually a sad back story as to why challenging people are the way they are.

17. A lack of skills

Making and building friendships requires a range of skills, including having the confidence to meet and be sociable with people, together with listening, assertiveness, time management, and organisational skills. Plus, knowing how to meet people, make friends, nurture nourishing relationships, demonstrate you care, and say 'no' to people. You will discover how to make friends in Part 2 of this book, and other useful skills to develop in Part 3.

18. Low self-esteem or confidence

How you feel about yourself affects many aspects of friendship, e.g. trying something new or speaking to people. However, most people aren't born with a lack of self-esteem or confidence, or social anxiety. These are learned beliefs, patterns of behaviours, and feelings. And thankfully, there are many ways to learn how to be more confident in social settings.

I used to be so shy and unsure of myself that I wouldn't say anything to anyone unless they spoke to me first. It's only through life experience, reading books, and attending many personal development courses over the years that I've become the confident person I am today. And you can do the same. Check out books or courses on how to be more confident – they could transform your friendships and life in so many ways.

I share how to develop a positive friendship mindset in Chapter 10, and how to manage your emotions in Chapter 17, so you can let go of social anxiety and say 'yes' to more friendship opportunities.

19. Not having much money

At my events, a lack of money is often given as a reason for not having many friends. And there's no doubt it's harder to make friends or join in when you're on a tight budget, need to work long hours to survive, or don't have the same disposable income to spend as those around you. This is often made worse if you live remotely with poor low-cost travel options or where the cost of participating in activities to meet new people is prohibitive.

That said, while money can make life easier and give you more choices, it doesn't guarantee happiness or friends. And there are plenty financially well off people who are lonely. Likewise, there are financially poor yet happy people who have good friends.

If money is tight, consider free and low-cost activities you could do to keep up with and make new friends – especially those that mean you can spend time with people for not much more than staying at home. Also consider how you could create even a little time or money to spend doing something regularly with people who could become friends.

~

During the Covid-19 pandemic, a friend mentioned how the restrictions around where we could go to meet people reminded her of some of her fondest and earliest memories of good times with friends and family. She talked about how much simpler things seemed when she was younger. Having less money and with fewer entertainment options available, much of her childhood was spent having fun outside, often doing things that didn't cost much money, e.g. picnics, sitting around a bonfire, playing rounders, paddling in the sea, going for walks, or sitting outside in the park with a cuppa from a flask. Another favourite activity later in life was having friends round for dinner where everyone brought a dish.

Whatever your financial situation, read this book through the filters of, what could be possible or adapted for your personal situation.

20. Living remotely

When you live remotely, face-to-face friendships can be more challenging. I used to live on a farm, so I know it takes more effort to make friends and see people. However since moving into a village, I've found it much easier. Nowadays, technology can help you to make or stay in touch with friends. So if you live remotely, consider what you could do to make friendships easier.

21. People change

This could be you or your friends. With all the lifestyle choices we have today, it's not surprising we all change throughout life – our values, priorities, interests, and how we want to spend our time. The reality is that most people we meet are not destined to be lifetime friends.

That's why it's so important to keep nurturing friendships and meeting new people throughout your life. Failing to do so could result in you having fewer friends as you get older.

What part have you played in having few friends?

This chapter highlights just some common reasons adults have no friends. Of course there are other reasons too, including racism, ageism, sexism, religious intolerances, all forms of prejudice, not being able to speak the same language as those around you, or being in a minority group.

Some of these reasons are circumstantial, e.g. persecuted refugees needing to flee their homes to survive which results in them being split up from family and friends. However, some reasons contributing to your lack of friends are likely to also be as a consequence of decisions you've made in the past. Thankfully, whatever your friendship experience so far, there are likely to be things you can do to make new friends and you will discover how to do so in this book.

In order to work out the best way for you to make and keep good friends in the future, first acknowledge which of these reasons resonate with you.

Key points

- If you have few friends, you're not alone. The upside of this is that there are lots of like-minded people waiting to meet you.

- Having an awareness of why you don't have many friends can help you accept limitations in your circumstances, while also highlighting changes you can make to enjoy good friendships.

- Making friends with people in a similar situation, or with people who don't have many friends, can be easier than trying to break into established friendship groups.

- Continuing to do what you've done in the past, without any changes, just turns your reasons into excuses that will sabotage future relationships.

Activity: Which of the above reasons resonates with you the most? Note these down in your journal and keep these in mind as you continue to read through the book.

Chapter 2
Why Friends Matter

Friends influence who you become: choose them wisely

I received a lovely text from a former client, when she heard I was writing this book. When we'd met, she didn't have many friends she could relate to and she was unsure how to handle friendship challenges. Through my Nourishing Friends course and coaching calls she completely turned things around. Here's what she said:

~

'I want to let you know about changes in my friendships. I've become really good friends with the person I run with, which has given me so much confidence. I can be myself completely, and she is open to telling me I'm appreciated. I've also been to see a film with a neighbour and asked her to join me at a local food festival. She was delighted. We both mentioned it to other friends and four of us ended up going.

I'd never have done that before or have looked forward to going out with these women. On top of that, we had friends for dinner last weekend and more are coming tonight. Thank you for your support, wise words, and insights that have brought me to this place.' Jane

Friendships enrich our lives in so many ways, impacting us emotionally and physically, opportunities we wouldn't otherwise hear about open up – when we're surrounded by the right friends. Medical studies also show friendships can help us live longer, so let's explore some of the key reasons they matter.

1. Improve your physical health

Your friends have a massive influence on your physical health, so choose them wisely if you want to enjoy good health and to increase your longevity.

People naturally gravitate towards people who are like them. If you're surrounded by friends who adopt healthy behaviours such as eating well, getting plenty of sleep, or you participate in physical activities together, you're more likely to adopt similar healthy habits too. However, if most of your friends want to go out and get drunk all the time, eat an unhealthy diet, or rarely exercise, you may do the same to fit in with them.

Unfortunately, it's not uncommon for people to selfishly mock or pressure friends to do something they don't want to do, such as having a drink or a slice of cake. When someone does this, they do it to make themselves feel better, but in doing so, they disrespect you. A good friend doesn't do this. They respect and support your choices without imposing their preferences.

Social isolation also affects physical health, especially as we age, and that's why friendships can be a protective essential ingredient for health, alongside eating well, sleeping, and movement.

2. Boost your mental and emotional well-being

Your friends also influence your mental health and how you feel.

Of course, that's not to say friends can fix everything. But sharing experiences, laughter and tears with friends, improves your overall emotional well-being. Good friends listen and help you talk through challenges, stress, and anxieties, no matter how they are feeling. They also encourage you to do things that help you cope better and feel good, rather than make you feel worse.

Emotions are infectious and create a ripple effect of feelings. When you surround yourself with happy people, their positivity can uplift your spirits. Conversely, being around people who are critical of you, manipulate or are negative towards you or life, will mean you are more likely to feel down, stressed, or miserable. That said, those grappling mental illness or going through a hard time are still valuable friends to have and may need your support – as long as they don't mistreat you.

Choose friends who make you feel good, and protect yourself against negative energies so that you don't get dragged down.

3. Live longer

Studies show that people with strong social ties, who are well integrated into their local community and have a good support network of friends, tend to live longer than those with no friends or who are socially isolated.

An ongoing Harvard study of adult development that's been running since 1938, reports that relationships with family, friends, and community, and the level of satisfaction you have with relationships in midlife, contributes more to your longevity than genetics and long-lived ancestors.[1]

When people experience a significant health event, it's easier to recover with the love, help, and support of family and good friends. One study suggests that in such situations, having a good circle of friends and being integrated into your local community could increase your chances of recovery by up to 50%.[2]

Good friends can also provide an invaluable sense of connection, purpose, and new opportunities as we age.

---

1. Find out more here - https://news.harvard.edu/gazette/story/2017/04/over-nearly-80-years-harvard-study-has-been-showing-how-to-live-a-healthy-and-happy-life/
2. Robin Dunbar, 2021, *Friends: Understanding the Power of our Most Important Relationships*, page 5.

4. Feel better supported

Life is certainly easier when we have a strong support system to help us navigate our way through all the twists and turns of life.

Friends can be invaluable in supporting us during challenging times, helping us celebrate in good times, and encouraging us as we embark upon new ventures or goals. Good friends show up to listen to you, and offer advice and help so you can cope better with whatever is going on in your life. Sometimes it's emotional support. Other times they may offer practical help, e.g. when you're physically ill or recovering from an operation. Local friends can rally around to assist with practicalities such as medical appointments, cooking, and being a valuable support to help you recover, while friends living further afield can provide critical emotional support.

Ask people for help when you need it. Most people will be pleased to be asked and doing so may also make it easier for them to ask you for help when they need it too.

5. Enjoy a deeper sense of connection, meaning, and belonging

Regularly spending time with close friends reduces feelings of loneliness, especially when you're part of a loving, supportive group or community bonded by shared interests, causes, or life experiences.

Having good local friends you can meet face-to-face strengthens feelings of connection and belonging. If you live remotely or have other physical restraints, keeping in touch with friends online is preferable to having no contact with the outside world. Similarly, actively participating in and contributing to your local community offers opportunities to make friends and experience a profound sense of belonging and purpose.

6. Improve your self-esteem

In my opinion, one of the most significant roles of being a good friend is to help each other to feel good. Through offering positive feedback and reassurance, friends have the power to remind us of our inherent worth and capabilities. A conversation I had with a good friend about a challenge I'd faced recently proved to be incredibly uplifting. Hearing her validate my thoughts affirmed my belief that I had made the right decision. And her words of encouragement not only boosted my confidence but also made me feel better about myself.

7. Cope better

Following on from all the above points, good friends can help us to cope better when facing life's challenges. They can offer tips or new strategies for dealing with difficult situations. And simply having someone to talk to can often make all the difference.

8. Gain a broader perspective

Friends often come from different backgrounds and have diverse experiences and perspectives. When you are open to listening to others and embracing diversity, this can broaden your horizons, challenge your beliefs, and help you to grow as an individual.

9. Enjoy more opportunities

I wonder if you've ever heard through a friend about a film, job, book, or event that's appealed to you? Or have you been introduced to a new friend, partner, or client through someone you know? You may even have heard about a job or business opportunity through a friend.

Good friends often share ideas, swap recommendations, and invite others to events. Each time they do this, they create opportunities you may not have otherwise heard about or experienced. They can provide valuable connections in both your personal and professional life, potentially opening doors to new experiences, friendships, and partnerships.

10. Have more fun and enjoy life more

Friends are companions with whom we can have fun, relax, and enjoy life. Engaging in leisure activities, hobbies, and adventures with them can create lasting memories and enhance our quality of life.

Let's beat the loneliness pandemic

It deeply saddens me that so many people are lonely and have stopped being sociable. A report issued in May 2024, states that nearly 60% of adults in the UK feel lonely some, often, or most of the time. Almost half of people over fifty reported feeling lonely often or most of the time.[3]

Age UK defines loneliness as a 'negative feeling people experience when the relationships they have don't match up to those they would like to have'.[4] But science indicates loneliness is far more than a feeling – it's an entire mind and body chronic stress state that triggers all sorts of symptoms including inflammation, struggling to sleep, brain fog, depression, feeling different or not good enough, and a range of other behaviours.

It's not surprising the World Health Organization considers social isolation and loneliness a serious threat to health and longevity that can increase your risk of early death by 25%, dementia by up to 50%, and cardiovascular disease by up to 33%.[5]

There are many reasons people can feel lonely, including unresolved trauma or abandonment issues from childhood, family and friends being absent or passing away, not feeling part of a family or community, not investing in friendships, not being able to participate in life in the way you'd like, or living alone or in a household with little meaningful connection.

As life expectancy increases, more older people will be living alone and at risk of loneliness – until we better embrace and value ageing and older people, and society offers more inviting, stimulating, and attractive communities and support services for older people.

---

3. The Centre for Social Justice Report: *The Lonely Nation*, May 2024, pages 5 and 9.
4. Age UK Report: *All the Lonely People: Loneliness in Later Life*. September 2018. https://www.ageuk.org.uk/globalassets/age-uk/documents/reports-and-publications/reports-and-briefings/loneliness/loneliness-report_final_2409.pdf
5. WHO Report, *Social Isolation and Loneliness Among Older People*, July 2021 - https://www.who.int/publications/i/item/9789240030749 And https://www.who.int/teams/social-determinants-of-health/demographic-change-and-healthy-ageing/social-isolation-and-loneliness

This is the perfect time

Friendship may not solve everything but is a powerful remedy for many of the problems we face in the world. That's why it's important to act now to make friends who will be there for you, and love and support you, as you do them.

This book is the gift that keeps on giving once you embrace what I outline and go on to share your love, friendship, and wisdom with others of all ages.

Don't wait until a better time to make friends. Now is the perfect time to connect with more people and nurture good nourishing friendships.

Key points:

- Friends are good for you when they provide emotional and practical support, boost how you feel, and help you enjoy yourself – all through life. They can even improve your health and longevity.

- The friendship benefits you experience, however, depend on your choice of friend. Good, nourishing friends will enrich your life. Poor friendship choices make your life worse. So choose your friends wisely. This is what you will learn how to do in this book.

- Now is the perfect time to start making more good friends – so you feel better, avoid feeling lonely in later years, and can make the most of life for years to come.

Activity: Reflect on what you're taking away from this chapter in your journal.

Loneliness support: If you are feeling lonely, isolated and need personal support, there are charities and groups all around the world that provide this. Do an internet search for loneliness support in your local area or go to see your local medical practitioner.

Chapter 3
Empowering Friendship Secrets

Your thoughts, feelings, and habits create your future friendships

There are ample opportunities for you to make friends and cultivate meaningful relationships, no matter your age or your life experience so far.

But are you ready to reap the countless benefits good friendships bring?

In this chapter I highlight the most enlightening 'ah ha' moments shared by participants during my friendship events and courses. These simple, yet liberating, insights profoundly influenced how they now approach friendships, and they are at the heart of many strategies I share in this book.

1. People with lots of friends are often initiators

Many people wanting more friends wait for invitations from others. Conversely, those with abundant friendships frequently take the lead, ask people out, and arrange group gatherings or outings. They prioritise friendship regardless of life's circumstances.

Your future friendships will reflect the small decisions and behaviours you make, starting from today.

Friendship tip #01: become an initiator

If you want more friends, ask more people out. Adopting this one new behaviour could make a huge difference.

Ask yourself, what holds me back from being more proactive and initiating plans? And imagine what could be better when you ask more people out.

Clients often cite fear of rejection as the main reason for not doing this. Inviting others out can make you feel vulnerable, as you're effectively declaring, 'I like you.' When people say 'no', some people mistakenly interpret this to mean the other person doesn't like them. However, this assumption may not be true.

There are a myriad reasons why people decline invitations. For example, they may lack the time to nurture new friendships or are too busy with existing family, work, or other commitments. I often meet people who could potentially be wonderful friends. But I barely have time to keep up with family and close friends. So, I'm one of those who often says 'no' simply due to a lack of time.

If you're held back by fear of rejection, remind yourself: the more people I ask out, the more friends I'll have. Of course, some might say 'no'. But if you choose the right people, some will say 'yes'. So aim for 'yes' and simply move on when people say 'no'. Consistently making this small change will expand your friendship circle.

2. The friends you attract reflect how you show up

We naturally attract people who share our perspectives, values, interests, or experiences. For instance, positive, proactive, and confident people gravitate towards friends who embody similar qualities, while avoiding those who are negative. Conversely, negative, critical, and insecure people often attract others who share similar beliefs and behaviours.

Similarly, introverts may find extroverts overwhelming, while extroverts might perceive introverts as challenging to engage with.

There is no right or wrong, but be aware that the person you are reflects the friends you attract. If you want relationships with people who will treat you with love, kindness, and respect, ensure that you embody these qualities too.

When you attract the right people, that's feedback that you're projecting your future friend's desires well. Of course, the opposite is true when you attract people you don't want as friends.

That's not to say you can't be friends with people who are very different from you. Of course you can. Having a diverse range of friends of all ages, races, backgrounds, cultures, interests, and personality traits, provides you with a richer perspective on the world.

But remember, what you talk about and how you interact with others influences whether you get a positive or negative response.

Friendship tip #02: be the friend you want to attract

When you are clear about the type of friends you want, and step into being this version of yourself, you will attract more of your ideal friends. Find out more about this in Chapters 6, 7, and 12.

3. Most friendships don't last forever

It's natural for friendships to come and go, with some being closer than others. Most people you meet are only destined to be in your life temporarily. Some friendships may not last long, while other people become lifelong companions, accompanying you through the twists and turns of life. In most cases, your friendship journey will be a unique assortment of friends and experiences.

I love this quote that sums up the fluidity of friendships: 'People come into your life for a reason, a season, or a lifetime.' – Brian A Chalker.

- **Reason** – these relatively brief connections offer valuable companionship, insights, or support, and no matter how fleeting, they can profoundly impact your well-being.

- **Season** – these relationships often last a specific phase of your life and then fade away, e.g. work colleagues, other parents you met when your children were young, or people going through a similar situation or experience to you. Though temporary, they often leave lasting impressions.

- **Lifetime** – lifetime friends are people with whom you share a mutual bond, desire, and commitment to maintain an enduring friendship. They add richness and help you navigate life with more joy, support, and confidence.

Losing touch with a friend doesn't mean that the friendship didn't work out: it's just a normal part of life. Lifelong friends are exceptional.

Friendship tip #03: accept the ebb and flow of friendships

Once you accept that most friendships are temporary, you'll find it easier to let some go and create space for new ones. As people drift in and out of your life, it's important to keep forming new connections, particularly as we grow older and more people around us die. So continue to make and nourish friendships all through life to lessen the likelihood of feeling isolated or lonely.

4. You're never too old to make friends

Attendees of my friendship events often said they thought they were too old to make new friends. But you're never too old to make new friends.

∾

One of my aunts recently told me about a powerful message one of my great-aunts shared while she was visiting her in a remote Scottish coastal village. With the yachts of a sailing school in view one morning, the family discussed the potential for my cousins to do some sailing lessons. One of my nephews said they didn't want to go because they wouldn't know anyone. My great aunt (in her late eighties at the time) responded, 'Oh, you mustn't let that stop you. Everyone you don't know is a potential new friend. I've just made a new friend. It's lovely to make friends.'

∾

Friendship tip #04: keep making new friends all through life

The nature of your friendships may change as you age, but human beings are social creatures who generally thrive better in company. Having friends around you as you age is vital if you want to make the most of life for as long as possible. Whatever your age, there are plenty of other people like you eager to have more friends. Rather than feeding the belief you're too old to make friends, I encourage you to work through this book so that you know how to find friends who will enrich this season of your life – with more confidence, ease, and joy.

5. Occasional arguments and conflicts are natural

Even with our closest friends, we're unlikely to agree on everything. During our lifetime, we all grow, change, and have very different life experiences. It's also human for us all to make mistakes and for emotional triggers from the past to cause unintentional upsets on either side of a friendship. I hate to think I unintentionally upset or hurt anyone, but the reality is that this is something we all do.

If you're lucky, though, your friends will tell you if you upset them so that you can have a chat, apologise, and move on – often with a stronger friendship. However, some people have a zero-tolerance policy and cut people out of their lives without any discussion or explanation. The downside of doing this could mean they're unnecessarily throwing away a good friendship.

Given that misunderstandings are common, I feel that cutting good friends off without a conversation is disrespectful. Like most people, I don't like conflict or having difficult conversations, but it's more important to me to give people the benefit of the doubt. I prefer exploring how we can resolve any issues or to agree to disagree... unless someone has significantly crossed the line.

Friendship tip #05: learn to avoid, resolve, and cope with conflict

Learning how to cope better with conflict is one of the most valuable skills to learn and apply in all walks of life. This involves developing several practical abilities so that you can prevent challenges from arising and find it easier to have uncomfortable conversations and let go of emotional upset, stress, and anxiety. I share tips for doing this in Chapter 21.

6. You make better friendships when you're selective

When we're young, our friendships are determined by circumstances, and are often influenced by our parents or carers, e.g. where we live and the school we attend. We probably fell into these friendships with little conscious thought, but if we're lucky, some of these friendships will continue and evolve throughout our lives. Unfortunately, many people follow the same patterns as adults. They fall into circumstantial superficial friendships and then wonder why they don't have many friends they can fully trust or have meaningful conversations with.

Friendship tip #06: be intentional as you invest in friendships

Clarifying the type of friends you want, and then regularly setting aside time to keep in touch with them, will yield more life-enriching friends and memorable experiences.

You deserve to be surrounded by fabulous friends who love you as much as you do them. So remember to select your friendships wisely and tend them with positive intention.

7. No friend can satisfy all your needs

I remember someone telling me she'd made some new friends but was yet to find the type of friends she was really looking for – people who completely got her. She enjoys walks and going to the local coffee shop with her friends, but none of them are interested in having deep and meaningful conversations on topics of interest to her. She expected good friends to mirror her completely until I pointed out that no one person can ever satisfy all our needs. Since then she's much better at enjoying the good qualities of friends, while accepting their limitations too.

The same can be said for friendship groups. If you're looking to find your tribe or community, you could be setting yourself up for disappointment if you are looking for one group that will satisfy all your needs all through your life. Instead, explore being part of several friendship groups.

Friendship tip #07: have friends for different reasons

Often, friends will satisfy a range of needs and aspirations, while some you may only see for a certain activity. Both types of friends are perfect as long as you both enjoy your relationship and time together.

When you accept you can have friends for different reasons, you can focus on making friends, individually or through groups, who will each fulfil specific needs. Collectively, all these new friends will enrich your life.

8. People who regularly mistreat you are not good friends

In Chapter 6, I define nourishing friends versus unhealthy friendships. Good friends consistently treat you with love, kindness, and compassion. People who often mistreat you, e.g. put you down, hold you back, are abusive, or hurt you, are not good friends. Yes, you may understand the reasons why they are the way they are but that doesn't excuse them from using you as a punchbag.

Friendship tip #08: focus on friends who treat you well

This involves being selective about which relationships to nurture (see Chapter 15), and pausing or ending friendships that are not good for you (see Chapter 22).

9. Be friends with adults of all ages

There are huge benefits to having younger friends and older friends, at all stages of life. I was inspired by my gran who made friends with people of all ages. She even came to the travel club I set up when she was in her eighties – because she enjoyed connecting with like-minded people.

Friendship tip #09: don't be put off by an age gap

As you get older, the less age differences are relevant. What's more important is the level to which you connect and enjoy people's company. If you specifically want to meet older or younger people, consider where you could meet them.

10. Every moment is a choice point

Whatever your experience with friends in the past, you can create the type of relationships you yearn for. Every moment is a choice point. This includes: where to go, who to ask out, who to say 'yes' or 'no' to, how you show up, what you say, what you don't say, and much more.

Friendship tip #10: make smarter choices

Have you ever wanted one thing yet done the opposite? It's common to have unconscious beliefs and emotions that conflict with what you consciously want. The challenge is that your unconscious beliefs usually win the day unless you stop them. For example, you may want to say 'no' to someone, but you say 'yes' because you don't like letting people down or upsetting them. Yet sometimes, saying 'no' would be the best thing for you to do. Conversely, if you experience social anxiety and your automatic response is 'no', saying 'yes' more often could help you make more friends.

To make smarter friendship decisions, double check your initial response is aligned to what you really want at a conscious level. Then respond in a way that's aligned with your desire for good friends.

Key points:

- Be selective about who you choose to spend time with and ask more people out.

- The friends you attract reflect your actions and behaviours. Be the friend you want to have in the future.

- Most friendships don't last forever, so make new friends and nurture relationships with people of all ages, all through life.

- Conflict is natural, so learn how to cope with it when it arises and let go of friends who are not good for you.

Activity: Reflect on what you're taking away from this chapter in your journal.

Chapter 4
Types of Friends

It's good to have different types of friends

Understanding different types of friends and the natural evolution of friendships helps you to make good friendship choices.

We all have different interpretations of what a friend is. For some, it's someone to talk to or spend time with. For others, there needs to be a deeper connection, e.g. common values, shared interests, or an appealing energy, before they'd call someone a friend.

Social media, and Facebook in particular, has encouraged people to adopt a looser definition of friendship, with some people having friends they have never met in person or only met once or twice.

However, any formal definition of a friend doesn't really matter. What's more important is the type of person you consider a true friend, and what kind of relationship you want.

That said, in this chapter I share some friendship models so you have more clarity on the range of friendships and relationships that could contribute to your life.

Aristotle's three types of friendship

Aristotle split friendships into three categories: utility friends who are born from circumstances and who often serve a temporary purpose, e.g. friends you meet through school, university, work, neighbours, or a shared life experience; pleasure friends who are people you choose to be around, for as long as you have shared values, interests, or connections; and virtue friends being your closest friends and those you feel the deepest connection with. Utility and pleasure friendships often end once the shared experience is over, with only a few becoming close friends. You move on and make new friends and the cycle repeats itself throughout life.

'There are degrees of friendship. Your best friends are those who listen and share time with you, make you laugh, let you cry, and don't mind a few sleepless nights because you snore. There are other friends I do activities with, but I wouldn't necessarily ring them in times of strife. Valuing all degrees of friendship is key to me.' Misti

Dunbar's numbers

Renowned evolutionary psychologist Robin Dunbar has been studying the natural interactions of human groups and the social layers of small societies, since the 1990s. Together with scientists from around the world, he noticed that our relationships could be categorised into inclusive circles (where outer circles include the people in inner circles), with predictable numbers of friends or contacts in each. And so the concept of friendship circles, also commonly referred to as Dunbar's Numbers, was born.[1] In a simplified form, he talks about close friends in the inner circle who you see most often, then best friends, good friends, friends, and acquaintances – where the outer rings represent people you know and see the least.

---

1. To find out more about friendship circles, check out Robin Dunbar's book: *Friends: Understanding the Power of our Most Important Relationships*, 2021, p68.

Nourishing Friends Circles

The focus of this book is to encourage you to develop nourishing friends you will cherish for years – people you know, like, and trust, who treat you well and bring out the best in you. Love, appreciation, and connection are therefore at the heart of all meaningful nourishing friendships, as you'll discover in Chapter 6.

With this in mind, I invite you to consider this simple friendship model for your friendships, where all platonic friendships are infused with love and connection:

- **Good friends** – people you share a deep connection with and regularly make time for. The glue that bonds you is the depth of your friendship, and the way you keep in touch – in person, by phone, or online, whether or not you live near each other.

- **Social friends** – people you enjoy spending time with socially but who you don't connect with as deeply as your closest friends. Some of these may become close friends over time while others disappear from your life.

- **Acquaintances** – people you meet and like in the course of life e.g. through work, socially, or through friends. You talk to them but don't know them well. New friends start off as acquaintances. Some may develop into closer friendships but most will only be in your life temporarily. Unlike the usual definition of acquaintances, that includes all people you know whether or not you like them. I only include people I connect with – life is too short to maintain relationships with people I don't like (unless we're working on something together as part of a larger team, or they are part of an important friendship group). I don't need my brain or energy consumed by people I'd never be friends with.

Nourishing friends can move between these circles at different times of life, as long as the core ingredients of love and connection remain intact.

Good friends versus bad friends

As with all aspects of friendship, you can choose who to be friends with. When you start the process of reviewing friendships, you may realise that not all friendships are healthy relationships that deserve your time. Likewise, someone you've thought of as a close friend in the past may not necessarily be a good friend, e.g. if they constantly put you down or criticise you. In Chapter 6, you'll discover the difference between nourishing versus unhealthy friendships so you can make smart choices about who you want in your life.

Frequency versus level of connection

Some people think of their closest friends as those they see the most or turn to in a time of need. Others define close friends as those they feel the deepest level of connection with – the frequency of seeing them isn't as important as the level of connection they have.

~

I have good friends I used to see regularly but now only see occasionally, e.g. to go out for a meal, go on holiday, or visit each other. When we get together, it's like we've never been apart, thanks to the deep connection we forged in the past. The frequency of getting together isn't as important to me as my love and gratitude to these friends for being in my life.

~

Again, how you define good friends is up to you. I simply invite you to consider what's more important to you: the frequency you see a friend or the depth of your connection and friendship?

Quality over quantity

We all have different views on our ideal number of friends. Some people like to have a large circle of friends while others prefer a small, more intimate group of close friends.

Studies suggest we have a growing friendship group until around the age of thirty when it stabilises, before dropping off again from your sixties. However, this assumes that everyone meets more people when they are young rather than later in life. And that's not always the case. Increasingly women are choosing to discard outdated beliefs about ageing and retirement. Many are choosing to do something new and make the most of life irrespective of their age. This includes making new like-minded friends to join them on their new adventures.

Rather than aiming to have a certain number of friends, I encourage you to make friends all through life, be selective over your choice of friends, and have as many or few friends as you have the capacity to maintain. Be mindful though that close friendships take more time and effort than with those you only see at work, social events, or as part of a group.

Online friends

The past few decades have introduced a new type of friend: those we make, nurture, and maintain online.

I remember the first time I heard about someone referring to a person they'd only met and conversed with online as a friend. I'm not proud to say I was judgemental and questioned the quality of their friendship, simply because I hadn't experienced this type of friendship for myself. However, over the last 15 years, I've met and nurtured online contacts into friends. And now I appreciate the value of such friendships: they can enhance your life, especially if they don't live nearby or you're housebound.

I liken online friends to a modern form of penfriends, the key difference being the range of ways we can now have live conversations rather than exchanging handwritten letters. You may have friends where the whole relationship has been online. Or you may occasionally meet up with online friends in person.

One of the great benefits of the internet is how it enables us to easily keep in touch with people we don't live near. Likewise, when used well, it can also help us to deepen connections and feel a sense of intimacy or belonging, e.g. through small WhatsApp groups where members share a certain bond. Online friends can also be a great support, especially if you're going through something similar and don't have many local friends you can speak to about what you're experiencing.

The same friendship principles apply when meeting, nurturing, and maintaining online relationships. Albeit there are different security and communication skills to consider.

I have friends around the world with whom much of our friendship has been conducted online. We may have only met in person once or twice, but we've maintained the relationship online. Are they friends or acquaintances? To me, if I feel a deep connection and love socialising with them outside work, I think of them as friends.

The evolution of friendships

All friendships go through a similar cycle: you meet people, get to know each other, and then a friendship flourishes – if you both think you're a good fit and make time for each other:

1. Getting to know people

As we get to know people we start to determine whether we could become friends. Even in situations where you click immediately, it can still take time to know people well. How quickly this happens depends on how comfortable you feel in each other's company, the time you invest in the friendship, and the extent to which you both want to be good friends. It also depends on your mindset, emotional resilience, and friendship skills. Just like dating, making friends is a journey of discovery. Along the way, you'll find some friends and people it's best to let go.

2. Nurturing friendships

Just like plants, all friendships need love and attention. Making and maintaining good friendships takes time and effort. Failure to nurture relationships, even when you know someone well, can cause friendships to drift apart.

We all have different attitudes towards how we like friendships to evolve. No matter how busy you are, making time to stay in touch with people you care about makes all the difference. I spend time every week, every month, and every year considering who to get in touch with. And I reach out to family and friends on a constant cycle.

3. Letting people go

It's natural for you not to like or click with everyone, and for others to feel the same about you, too. You might determine this quickly, although in the early stages of a relationship, people are often on their best behaviour. It can take months or years for some people to show their true colours through undesirable behaviours or clashes of values or opinions.

Whenever you decide you don't want to be friends with someone, give yourself permission to end the friendship or let it fizzle out naturally. It allows you to free yourself from future strife and have more time to spend with people you like. I share tips on how to end friendships in Chapter 22.

'I used to take things personally when friendships ended. But having done Alisoun's Nourishing Friends course, I now know that when I drift apart from friends, it's not because either of us has done something wrong. Rather, when a friendship has passed its prime, we're simply no longer on the same journey together. We came together for a certain period in our lives, as we had something to share. Then, as is normal for many friendships, we went our separate ways. There is no blame or fault. It's about accepting and surrendering to the process of life. Yes, I may still feel sadness when a friendship ends. But I no longer feel any blame or shame.' Julie

Accepting changes in your friendships

All friendships are an evolving dance in response to life events. Some friendships flow easily and will last a lifetime. However, others will have a limited lifespan. Likewise, a friend can move from being an acquaintance to being one of your inner social circle, and vice versa.

Holding onto the belief that you need to be able to maintain a friendship all through life sets you up for disappointment and sometimes feeling that you're not a good friend.

Yet the reality is we all change through life. Nothing is permanent – including friendships.

Treat finding good friends like dating

Do you apply a similar intentional approach to making friends as you do to finding a partner or soul mate?

Look at the effort that goes into finding the right life partner. Some people are lucky to meet them with little conscious effort, e.g. through friends, work, or chance meetings. However, that's not the case for everyone, and nowadays many people meet their partners through dating apps. To get the most from these, you define your desired qualities for partners and include these in your profile. Then you date compatible people. Sometimes you see people several times to decide if they're a good fit. You may hope each person could be the love of your life but you actually rule many people out.

In the same way this filtering process is an acceptable way to find romantic partners, it can be applied to making friends too. When building relationships with people, you may realise some are not for you. This is not a failure on your part, and it's totally acceptable to walk away from relationships with people you don't resonate with or to end friendships that are not good for you.

One thing that's different with platonic relationships is that it's unlikely one person will be able to satisfy all your friendship needs. That's why it's healthy to have a range of friends and a mix of types of friendships.

Feel a sense of belonging through friendship groups

The focus so far has been on individual friendships. However, also consider friendship groups too – especially if you're eager to find your tribe or feel you belong in a group. The need to belong to a group or community is a primal human trait. We are social beings and a species that has survived partly due to us faring better when we're part of a group.

For years, I watched people be a part of groups who bonded at university or through having children. And if I'm honest, I was jealous. Yes, through setting up a travel club and business networking groups, I felt I belonged in these groups. But they were large groups of people, many of whom I didn't socialise with. Then, during the Covid-19 pandemic, I felt that deep sense of community and belonging for the first time – when I started sea swimming with a group of women. The unique bonds, connections, and conversations we had each time we came together on the beach, activated something special in my heart.

So, how do you find this sense of belonging? If you're fortunate enough to feel part of a group where you feel a deep sense of belonging, e.g. your family, community or group of friends, then savour this. It's something most of us yearn for, yet it can often prove elusive.

My experience of friendship groups has given me these insights:

- Joining existing groups or clubs based around an activity you enjoy or would like to try can be fruitful.

- You feel a sense of belonging when you feel safe to turn up as the authentic you and not pretend to be someone else.

- We can enjoy a sense of belonging in a range of different groups. As with individual friendships, it's unlikely that one group will satisfy all your needs. You probably have more than one 'tribe', so have fun experiencing and joining a range of different groups.

- When we're part of a group, we may not connect to everyone. Yet we can still feel a sense of belonging.

- Bringing together a group of people and organising regular events is a good way to create your tribe and to feel a deep sense of belonging – especially if you socialise with them.

Key points

- Adopt a proactive approach to making friends as you would when seeking a life partner, while still being open to spontaneity and the most unlikely of friendships.

- Be intentional about the friendships you make, nurture, and rekindle. You'll be exploring this in Section 2.

- Be mindful that the type of friends you want in the future may differ from those you've had in the past. Focus on the people you need and want in your life.

- If you yearn for a sense of belonging, join or create a group of like-minded people.

Activity: Reflect on what you're taking away from this chapter in your journal.

Chapter 5
Friendships As We Age

Friendships evolve and change all through life

In this chapter, I focus on how friendships evolve as we age. These insights come from a mix of personal experience, working with clients, doing research, and collecting feedback from older women.

I'm conscious that looking at friendships purely from an age perspective is a huge generalisation and could be viewed as ageist. Other factors at play can mean your experience of these stages could be very different. Especially if you feel you don't fit into society's norms, you are an introvert, suffer from health challenges, or have different cultural expectations.

I'm also aware that much of what I share comes from a place of privilege – in terms of race, education, and the opportunities I and many others enjoy in the Western world, e.g. having the freedom to work, earn money, and be an independent woman.

However, I do feel it's important to understand the impact common life events have on most of us to some degree. As you read through this and following chapters, I invite you to put what I share into the context of your own personal circumstances and life.

Young children

Young children develop kinship friendships with people they can play and have fun with. In our younger years, we don't have much concept of what a friend is, often playing independently alongside other children. As we get older, we start to consider people we like spending time with regularly, as a friend. However, it takes a few more years to understand the depth of a mutually beneficial friendship and what this involves.

Childhood friendships are often based on our parents' friends and their ideas about how they'd like our lives to be. If you had absent parents, suffered neglect, lived remotely, or had parents who didn't socialise much, you may have missed out on these curated friendships.

Occasionally, special bonds are created at a young age that endure through life, although this is the exception, not the norm.

Think back to when you were young. Did you meet people, e.g. at school, clubs, or social gatherings organised by your parents? Whether or not you found it easy to make friends in these settings, you were nevertheless likely to be meeting people. Those early friendship experiences unconsciously influence your adult friendships, unless you take conscious action to heal from any trauma, bullying, or difficult situations you endured.

Early teens

Teenagers often have increasing autonomy over aspects of life, including their choice of friends. They are exposed to new people and experiences, both at school and socially. Yet for as long as your parents or carers had a large influence over you – e.g. where you lived – the pool from which you could select friends was still limited.

Adolescent brains are still maturing and their emotional intelligence still evolving, and many become more self-conscious. So, it can take time to recognise true friendship as mutually beneficial, and a very different relationship to what we've had with parents, family, and carers.

With all the changes that happen personally and socially, it's not surprising that teenage friendships can be ever-changing and sometimes turbulent.

Young adults

This is when most of us have more control and influence over the people we meet and choose to spend time with. At this stage, we're also still developing culturally appropriate social skills that will enable us to thrive as adults.

It's a time of experimentation, when it's common for those who prioritise friendships to make lots of friends through work, education, and hobbies. Typically, these start as utility acquaintances or pleasure friends to enjoy a certain period of your life with. But you may also pick up a few close lifelong friends along the way.

Your late twenties and thirties

As the years go by, the desire to meet a life partner often becomes stronger, and friendships change as a consequence. Many people prioritise dating and spending time with potential partners over friendships. Likewise, friendship circles can also shrink as careers, working long hours, and family commitments become a priority.

'Friends when you were young were chosen because of coincidence: through being at school, university, or work. But as you get older, you're more certain of who you are and seek people that bring you joy. Sometimes people do let you down, either by gossiping or not backing you in difficult times – it's such a shock. But like a paper boat, let go and watch it leave...' Glenda

Other life experiences also have a significant impact on friendships, both positive and negative, including marriage, divorce, becoming a parent, being involuntarily childless, moving somewhere new, having health issues, caring for parents, and the loss of loved ones.

Each change in circumstance presents the possibility that some friendships will ebb away while also introducing you to new people. However, you can maintain good friendships throughout life, especially with friends you have a deep connection or bond with, though it may take more effort, or the nature of your friendship may change.

Midlife years

Friendships in your midlife years flow through a revolving door. Some friends will continue the journey of life with you, while others drift away. You meet new friends as your work and personal circumstances continue to change. Juggling family and work commitments often becomes more challenging at this stage of life, and so friendships can suffer – unless you make time for them.

~

Personally, my thirties were my loneliest years as most people around me started having babies. I desperately wanted children, but that wasn't to be. It was upsetting to be excluded from the elusive parent club. My upset was compounded by people continually judging and criticising me because I didn't have children – shockingly, the meanest were new mums. Thankfully, as soon as I decided to start seeking out other childless friends, I felt a lot better.

~

People who are good at maintaining friendships find it easier than others to navigate their way through this stage of life. However, many people in their midlife years find they have fewer friends than they once had or are questioning some of their friendships.

The internet can play an increasing role in maintaining relationships as we age, especially with people who have moved away, have limited time, or are not as mobile as they once were. But it can also make you feel that others are enjoying life more than you – until you accept that what you see is usually only a tiny snapshot of their lives and there's likely to be more going on than you see.

Your fifties, sixties, and beyond

This is often a time when we go through several life transitions, e.g menopause, retirement, children leaving home, friends and family passing away more frequently, or becoming a carer to sick or ageing family or friends. Such events often prompt us to re-evaluate our life, friendships, and to make changes. I share a collection of insights from women over sixty on their friendship tips for life, retirement, and ageing in Chapter 24.

Common themes include being more discerning about the people they choose to spend time with, feeling more confident about saying what they think, standing up for themselves, and not tolerating undesirable behaviours. Some mentioned caring responsibilities being a factor that can get in the way of friendships, in a similar way parenting does for younger people. But others talk about the fun and joy they have with new friends as they embrace new adventures together now that they have more time to make the most of life.

~

'Cherish your female friends as you'll enjoy their company so much as you get older and benefit from their wisdom and shared experience. Our bodies and thoughts about life change as we go into our sixties and sharing these changes and insights with other women is so helpful. We can also have a lot of fun times!' Elizabeth

~

Retirement

In some ways, friends in retirement are even more important than at any other stage of life – especially if you've stopped working, are single, live alone, don't have children or family nearby, or have mobility limitations.

Remember, good friendships boost your health and longevity, including your cognitive function, and can help you feel a sense of connection, meaning, and belonging. All of which will help you to live an independent life for longer. But only if you choose your friends wisely.

As you grow older, your friendship circles are likely to continue to evolve and reflect your changing needs, interests, and approach to life. Typically maintaining your health, remaining independent, and bucket list goals become both priorities and opportunities to make new friends.

Just like all other stages of life, your friendships in retirement depend upon your personal circumstances and how much time you invest in them. For example, if you're the first in your group of friends to retire, you may need to spend more time making new friends compared to someone who already has lots of retired friends. Most of those I spoke to said retirement improved their friendships, giving them more time to have fun with friends and reconnect with people they hadn't seen for a while.

Choices people often face in retirement that impact friendships include:

- **Changing needs** – many of your needs such as connection, meaning, or belonging can come from work, so when you retire you might need to be more proactive in making friends to have these needs met. This may involve needing to find people who are available during the day, new ways to fill your days, or activities to keep fit or stimulate your brain. You could get involved in your local community through classes, social clubs, or volunteering. The internet has also been pivotal in enabling some older people to keep in touch with people they wouldn't otherwise see.

- **Working in retirement** – increasingly people are continuing to work in some capacity in retirement, either because of financial necessity or through choice, e.g. to enjoy social interaction and connection, or add meaning or purpose to their life. The type and intensity of work often changes, e.g. you may give up a career and then work part-time doing something completely different or set up a small business. Being able to continue to work and engage with others for as long as you need or want is a privilege many people don't have.

- **Precious time** – there is no doubt that the fragility of life becomes more acute as we grow older. I was speaking to a friend recently about how when friends died when I was young, I still felt invincible, that I still had most of my life ahead of me. Yet, I've noticed feeling very different since my dad died a couple of years ago. He was only 25 years older than me, and I'm far more conscious that I want to cram as much as I can into the next twenty years of my life, before I feel less inclined or able to do so. Not in a morbid way, but rather a motivator for me to make smarter choices about how I spend my time, including who I spend it with.

- **Bucket list adventures** – do you have things you'd love to do or see before you die? Create a bucket list and explore how you can work through this, possibly with friends. Sometimes merely mentioning to someone what you'd love to do can spark a conversation or trip together. Or there are likely to be events or groups you could join where you could meet new like-minded people.

~

'Make sure you have male friends too. Men have had a lot of bad press in the last few years, but some of the most important and supportive people I know are men. I am lucky enough to have lovely, kind, caring male friends – with whom I have had the most touching and heartfelt conversations and great support. Men need kind, caring women to talk to as well. We have a divide now which needs bridging – which maybe needs healing.' Yvonne

~

- **Evolving friendship circles** – your wisdom years seem to be a time when people reassess friendships. Of the people who completed my friendship survey, 42% were over fifty. Of these, 10% said they didn't like or relate to some of their friends any more. Friends moving away, becoming less mobile, or dying, can create deep sadness and holes in the lives of those left behind. This is one of the main reasons why making and maintaining friendships all through life is so important.

- **Local support** – older women who completed my survey shared how important it is to have local friends for company, to help each other out practically, and to check in on one another regularly. It seems the more homebound or physically limited we are, the more important able-bodied local friends become.

- **Caring responsibilities** – caring for others can get in the way of friendships at any stage of life, whether as a parent or caring for an ill or ageing relative or friend. With more older people living alone, caring for friends, checking in on them, and supporting each other is increasingly part of friendship.

~

'I've been part of a friendship group for the last thirty years. Despite moves and changes in how we communicate, we're still committed to meeting on Zoom every month. We support each other in choosing the higher vibrations and hold each other in our meditations/prayers until the following month. There are four of us, aged 67, 82, 89 and 94. We've not missed a month in all that time.' Connie

~

- **Your mindset** – as with all other stages of life, you can choose how to approach life and ageing. You could see it as a privilege many people don't get the chance to experience, and focus on what you could do to make the most of life, for as long as possible. Or give in to outdated beliefs about ageing and focus on what you no longer have, and what's wrong with your body and life now. The choice is yours – for as long as you have the mental capacity to do so.

Key points

- Creating meaningful friendships is like discovering hidden treasures that brighten our lives, especially as we age.

- Make nourishing friends now to avoid feeling lonely in the future and help others around you feel better too. Keep reading to find out how to do this.

- Age is not the determining factor in whether you have friends. Rather it's your personal circumstances, mindset, and how you make, connect, and support friends all through life.

Activity: Reflect on what you're taking away from this chapter in your journal.

Chapter 6
Nourishing Friends Versus Unhealthy Friendships

Life is short, so spend it with nourishing friends

What kind of friends do you want?

When I ask people this, they usually list qualities such as people who are kind, like-minded, thoughtful, fun, supportive, non-judgmental, interesting, have a good sense of humour, or other positive behaviours and personality traits. No-one has said they were looking for friends who are bitchy, negative, abusive, self-centred, aggressive, possessive, rude, toxic, drama queens, or people who play the victim all the time.

Yet I wonder if you've ever found yourself in a relationship that made you unhappy. One where you look back and can see the red flags you ignored.

Knowing the signs of a healthy, nourishing friendship versus toxic behaviours will help you to be more selective of the friendships you pursue or avoid. Having this wisdom can also help you pull back from relationships that are not good for you.

The focus of this book is to help you make and enjoy fabulous nourishing friendships, rather than putting up with unhealthy friendships. So, what are nourishing friends?

Nourishing friends

Nourishing friends are people who are consistently good to you and enrich your life. Loyal friends who act with love, kindness, and positive intention. They're not just there for the good times, but also support you through challenging times. Nourishing friends:

- Want what's best for you.
- Help you feel better when you're feeling down.
- Are kind to you and respect you.
- Have other friends and ways to get their needs met.
- Do things that show they care and value your friendship.
- Take full responsibility for their actions.
- Say they are sorry when they make mistakes.
- Believe in you.
- Are encouraging, supportive, and celebrate your success.
- Are energising to be around.
- Make you feel better about yourself.
- Enjoy good laughs and conversations.
- Are open-minded and see things from different perspectives.
- Respect your values, views, and decisions.
- Help you navigate your way through life's challenges.

Sometimes nourishing friends make mistakes. However, they have the empathy, compassion, and confidence to apologise when they get things wrong – if you let them know when they upset you. In this book, we'll explore the critical qualities of a nourishing friend for you so you can make smart friendship choices.

～

One of my closest friends I'm sure is one of my gran's soul sisters. I was very close to my gran, who died just before I met this friend – another holistic, vegetarian, animal lover and activist. We clicked immediately and launched a successful holistic business venture within three weeks of meeting each other. She was my first business buddy, and over twenty years later she is still one of my most cherished friends.

Unhealthy friendships

There are some people who are not good for your mental health or physical well-being. They often make you feel worse about yourself and sabotage your life.

Sometimes these people are referred to as 'toxic friends', although I feel this label is overused and misused to describe people who display even the smallest negative behaviour or a one-off indiscretion. Even good friends can have one or two undesirable behaviours or occasionally act out of character. Let's face it, none of us are perfect. Likewise, people frequently refer to individuals as narcissists without full awareness of this personality disorder.

You're in an unhealthy friendship when the other person consistently:

- Wants what's best for them, not you.
- Puts you down to make themselves feel better.
- Is mean to you, uses you, or abuses you.
- Is needy, possessive, or jealous.
- Doesn't show they care for you.
- Blames others and life events for what's wrong with their life – it's never their fault.
- Thinks they're right and rarely apologises.
- Dims your light and holds you back.
- Squashes your dreams.
- Drains your energy.
- Makes you feel worse about yourself, or causes unnecessary stress, anxiety, or worry.
- Is negative or critical.
- Bitches, moans, and gossips about people.
- Doesn't consider others' perspectives.
- Wants you to compromise your needs or integrity for their sake.
- Belittles the challenges you face.

If you recognise any of your friendships as unhealthy, I encourage you to consider whether you want to continue to be in it (with boundaries to protect you) or to end the friendship.

Unhealthy friendships versus good friends having a bad time

Supporting someone through a bad time is part of being a good friend – as long as they are still kind and respectful to you.

There's an important difference between being a good friend who is struggling versus someone who is consistently negative, critical, plays the victim, or mistreats or manipulates you into supporting them.

If you're a good friend who is usually kind and loving but are going through a tough time, friends will stand by you and support you. However, if you frequently overstep boundaries, engage in toxic behaviours, or mistreat others, you may find they are not there for you when you need them the most.

Emotional blackmail

I was speaking with someone recently who was being manipulated by a friend. Her friend was using an illness as justification for being mean and saying nasty things about her – despite these being common behaviours before she got ill. With hindsight, my friend now realises that they'd never had a good friendship.

As with romantic partnerships, it can be really hard to pull back or walk away from friends you care about, particularly when you still love them and they're not in a good place. And it feels kinder to be more tolerant of people who are facing challenges in their lives such as mental illness, PTSD, chronic or critical illnesses, addictions, or dementia.

These may indeed be valid reasons for a friend's behaviours, but none justify abuse – whether verbal, emotional, or physical, and particularly if you feel threatened or in danger. That said, where you've chosen to take on a carer role for a friend, it may be reasonable to accept otherwise undesirable behaviours driven by their condition – but make sure you take care to protect yourself and ensure your own needs are met. To do this, set and affirm boundaries. I explain how to do this in Chapter 19.

How to avoid being in an unhealthy friendship

Friendships are a two-way dynamic. Your choice of friends and how you show up influences the quality of your friendships.

If you want to avoid unhealthy friendships, be selective about the friends you make, and be clear on what you need and can contribute to your friendships. Also be alert for red flags that warn there could be trouble ahead and let the other person know if they overstep one of your boundaries. If you don't, it will increase the likelihood you'll have unhealthy friendships.

Sometimes pausing or ending a friendship is what's best for you. I share factors to consider first and how to do this in Chapter 21.

Never dim your light

When others are not in such a good emotional or mental place as us, a way of connecting and fitting in is to dim our own light. With a friend who you know is struggling, maybe you pretend things aren't going as well for you as they are.

∾

A friend once apologised for speaking about her children and grandchildren with me, as she's aware I'm unintentionally childless and she didn't want to upset me. While her intentions were well-meaning, I never want any of my friends to play down what's happening with their families. My response was to tell her she must never feel she can't speak to me about her family. Of course, if that was all she talked about or if I thought she was deliberately doing it to hurt me, that could damage our friendship. Thankfully, we have a good friendship, made better by our mindful, honest conversations.

∾

I know I've downplayed things going well in my life in the past, for fear of upsetting others who are less fortunate than me. And, of course, there are times when it's wise to hold back information and wait until a better time to share something, or to tone things down a bit temporarily. But continually dimming your light for the sake of others isn't healthy. A good friend will celebrate when things are going well for you, even when things are challenging for them. In fact, a true friend will be happier knowing you are doing well, even if they're having a tough time.

Key points

- You deserve to be surrounded by friends who will love and respect you as much as you do them.

- When you're aware of nourishing versus unhealthy friendships, you can be more discerning about the friends you make.

- The part you play influences the quality of your friendships. Letting people mistreat you is fuel for unhealthy relationships. If you don't like the way friends are treating you, speak up. Setting clear boundaries and standing up for yourself yields better friendships.

- How to get out of unhealthy friendships depends on how long you've been friends, the extent of harmful behaviours, the part they play in your life, and the support structures you have in place. See Chapter 21.

- Considering friendships similar to life partners can be useful, so that you can proactively nurture good friendships and end relationships that are detrimental to your well-being.

Activity: Reflect on what you're taking away from this chapter in your journal.

Chapter 7
How to Be a Good Friend

Cultivating good friendships is like tending to a garden – it takes time and effort, but the rewards are worth it

In a world where relationships can seem fleeting or superficial, the importance of genuine friendship deepens with each passing year. In midlife, nurturing authentic connections becomes not just a desire, but a vital aspect of living a happy, fulfilling life. As we navigate the complexities of the second half of life, having friends who truly get us and support us is invaluable. Here are ten simple tips for being a good friend.

1. Take responsibility for being a good friend

We all carry unique strengths, weaknesses, personality traits, and personal life experiences into our friendships. Part of being a good friend means understanding yourself and being your greatest supporter, so you can show up as the best authentic version of yourself.

Embracing the role of a good friend encompasses both the enjoyable and challenging aspects of friendship. It means taking responsibility for the part you play in friendship – your behaviours and efforts to connect. It also involves staying in touch, offering support, initiating meet-ups, extending apologies, having difficult conversations, gently encouraging friends to grow, and being forgiving towards yourself and others. And yes, it also means healing your trauma and emotional triggers, standing up for yourself, and letting go of friendships that are not good for you.

It's easy to take responsibility for things that go well. The greater skill is taking responsibility for the part you have played when things don't go as you hoped. But blaming others causes division, conflict, and upset. Taking responsibility can help defuse situations and is more likely to aid resolution. It can be the difference that determines whether a friendship will continue to flourish or die. There is always a part you've played, even if that's hard to admit. Examples include:

- I haven't made an effort with friends in the past.
- I didn't know what I could do differently.
- I chose to be in this friendship.
- I allowed this person to bully me, criticise me, or put me down.
- I've ignored the red flags.
- I should have got out of the friendship sooner.
- Because I care, I stepped into the shoes of a rescuer or fixer, rather than allowing them to forge their own journey.
- I could have thought more about what I wanted to say, rather than reacting so quickly.
- I was abrupt because I was tired/stressed.
- I made unfair assumptions and judgements.
- I didn't think about things from their perspective.
- While my intentions were good, I could have handled things better.
- I've chosen not to master useful skills.
- I don't want to heal from past traumas even if they negatively impact my friendships.

When something goes wrong, ask yourself: what part have I played in this happening? The intention of doing this is not to be critical or to slip into the blame game. Rather it's about acknowledging your contribution so you can learn from the experience, so you're more likely to avoid this type of situation in the future. Once you're clear on the part you have played, it's also easier to apologise if appropriate.

2. Focus on what you can control and influence

Focusing on what you can't control is what leads to negative emotions like stress, anxiety, nerves, or disappointment. However, when you concentrate on what you can control and influence, you're likely to feel better and enjoy healthier friendships.

You can't control how others think, feel, or act. All you can control (once you know how) are your thoughts, feelings, actions, and behaviours. When this becomes a new habit you'll likely experience better friendships.

Examples of what you can control when nurturing friendships:

- **Your thoughts** – all your beliefs including your self-belief and perceptions of the other person, as well as your assessment of the conversation or situation. I share how to develop a positive friendship mindset in Chapter 10.

- **Your feelings** – how you feel about yourself, the other person, and the potential for a future friendship. If you don't know how to manage your emotions naturally, see Chapter 17.

- **Your actions** – what you do or don't do, what you say, the questions you ask, what you share, and your responses, including whether you say 'yes' or 'no'. As well as how long you speak to people, expressions of agreement or disagreement, invitations to connect, suggestions for meeting up, and how you handle challenges.

- **Your behaviours** – this includes how you show interest or disinterest through your words, tone, body language, and interactions with others. For instance, maintaining appropriate eye contact (not staring), nodding in agreement, smiling warmly, adopting open body language (avoiding crossed arms), and directing your attention toward the person rather than looking over their shoulder – all contribute to your demeanour. Plus expressing calm, confidence, or interest, through your tone of voice.

Examples of what you can't control:

- **What others think** – about you and the topics you discuss.

- **What others feel** – about themselves, their perceptions of you, and whether they want to be one of your friends.

- **What others do** – how they treat and respond to you, generally, during, and after conversations.

- **How others act** – whether you bring out the best in them or inadvertently activate one of their emotional triggers.

The best thing to do in any situation with friends is to only focus on what you can control and influence. Whenever you feel bad about something that has happened between you and a friend, that's feedback you're focussing on that you can't control, there is something to address, or you have a belief or emotional trigger to clear.

You could be more influential

Most people have the potential to be more influential than they realise. There are two core ways to be more influential:

- **Learn new skills** – when you learn new skills, especially around your mindset, emotions, and behaviours, you can become more influencial when interacting with others. If you want people to respond to you more positively or treat you better, focus first on embodying these behaviours towards yourself and those you want to be friends with, and notice what's different.

- **Team up with others** – when you connect with people who have the same opinions as you, you can be more influential as a group. We see this happening ahead of all social change – people collaborating and working together for a common cause.

3. Act from a place of love, kindness, and compassion

Love is at the heart of all nourishing friendships, so endeavour to engage your heart and act from a place of love, kindness, compassion, integrity, respect, gratitude, and peace.

Letting friends know how much you love and appreciate them goes a long way in nurturing mutual appreciation and strengthening closer bonds, especially when you do this unexpectedly. You could thank friends for their company, contribution, or the positive impact they have on your life. Or for something specific they have done. There are many ways to do this, e.g. verbally, or by sending them an email, card, message, letter or gift.

Being of service to your friends through thoughtful acts of kindness or by being generous with your time and attention, also helps build connections with people – as long as you don't go overboard, which can be smothering. Even during challenging times, coming from a place of love, kindness, and compassion can do wonders for your relationships.

I cover all of this and how to make a difference, to yourself and others, in my book, *Heartatude, The 9 Principles of Heart-Centered Success*.[1]

4. Be the good friend you want others to be

Most people want friends who radiate love, kindness, and compassion – people who are beacons of honesty, trustworthiness, open-mindedness, authenticity, and unwavering integrity. These are the foundations of all meaningful relationships, with yourself and others. Being loyal, supportive, appreciative, dependable, forgiving, and showing you care are also common desirable friendship qualities. True friendship transcends judgment, expectation, and jealousy.

In good friendships, you feel safe openly expressing your thoughts, feelings, and experiences. If you find yourself holding back personal opinions or experiences, this may indicate you're still getting to know someone and gauging your level of trust in them. Or it could be a red flag that this person might not be good for you. Regardless, being the friend

---

1.   Alisoun Mackenzie, *Heartatude, the 9 Principles of Heart-Centered Success, 2015.*

you'd like them to be, and accepting who they are without judgement, is essential in any healthy friendship.

Marisa G. Franco offers a deep exploration of this in her book, *Platonic: How Understanding Your Attachment Style Can Help You Make and Keep Friends*[2] where she shares six practices: taking initiative, expressing vulnerability, pursuing authenticity, harmonising with anger, offering generosity, and giving affection.

5. Set and honour boundaries

We all have unique needs, desires, and emotional triggers. By setting up and applying healthy boundaries, you will increase the likelihood of your friends understanding your needs, wants, and limits, so they can find it easier to treat you with the love and respect you need and deserve. Doing this also reduces the potential for future conflict. Discover how to set and apply friendship boundaries in Chapter 19.

6. Be supportive and demonstrate you care

Being a good friend means being there to support friends whatever is happening in their lives. This involves celebrating their successes, achievements, and life's milestones, with joy and enthusiasm. But it also means being there to listen and offer practical support during challenging times. Being a consistent supporter strengthens friendship bonds.

There's a book called *The Five Love Languages*[3] that gives powerful insights into understanding and demonstrating love in relationships. The five love languages are: words of affirmation (what you say to each other); giving gifts; loving physical touch; giving time; and acts of service (doing something for someone). We often communicate our love to others by applying our preferred love language, but the secret to showing others you

---

2. Marisa G. Franco, PhD, *Platonic: How Understanding Your Attachment Style Can Help You Make and Keep Friends*, 2022.
3. Gary Chapman, 2001, *The Five Love Languages: How to Express Heartfelt Commitment to Your Mate*.

care is to communicate this using *their* love language. Practical ways to demonstrate you care for friends include:

- Be in touch regularly, e.g. daily, weekly, or monthly.
- Ask friends what they need or how you can help.
- Send friends cards to celebrate birthdays and life events.
- Offer your friends comfort or assistance when they're ill or going through a challenging time, e.g. increase your contact, get their shopping, or make meals for them.
- Have fun with random acts of kindness, e.g. sending flowers, gifts, or treating friends to a meal when they least expect it.
- Hug friends (only if they're someone who likes hugs).
- Offer to look after pets or their house when they're on holiday.
- Help friends tackle challenging tasks.
- Introduce them to people you think they'd get along with.
- Remember what is going on for friends by taking a note to follow up or to check in on them.
- Tell them you love or appreciate them.

There are also numerous ways to follow up on initial meetings, such as sending messages, emails, or cards, sending them helpful information relating to your conversation or making introductions.

Thoughtful gestures such as these show you cherish and value their presence in your life.

7. Learn to be a good communicator

Most conflicts come from a clash of values, communication styles, or behaviours. Too often, people fall out with friends because they feel hurt, upset, or annoyed with how they feel their friends have treated them. Yet, often, poor communication was a key factor.

Skilled communicators take responsibility for unintentionally hurting or upsetting people. They apologise and accept responsibility for the part they've played in the exchange – rather than blaming the other person. I share communication skills tips in Chapter 18.

8. Celebrate friends' successes

It's incredibly uplifting when those around you are supportive and celebrate what's going well in your life. The same is true for your friends.

Celebrating friends' achievements, milestones, and moments of happiness with genuine enthusiasm, can deepen your friendship. Likewise, giving your friends encouragement, loving feedback, and space to evolve, grow, or pursue new goals, can strengthen your connection.

This can be hard when it feels like your friendship could change because of what your friend is doing, or when things aren't going well for you. However, in such moments, it's important to set aside any feelings of insecurity, loss, or envy.

~

One of the hardest things I've ever had to do was to express joy and excitement when a friend got pregnant, when I desperately wanted children too. Of course, I was really happy for my friends. But behind the scenes, I spent a lot of time in tears, devastated, although careful not to show it in their special moment of joy. Once I got over my initial upset, I was thankfully able to share their joy and enjoy time with their family.

~

9. Have fun and make the most of life together

Enjoying experiences, adventures, and activities together creates lasting memories and deepens friendships.

Seek out things you can do with friends. Planning activities together often creates new opportunities, helps you get to know each other better, and can forge stronger connections. Be inclusive by inviting people you know along to social activities or group gatherings. This helps to ensure friends feel valued, included, and part of your friendship circle.

Infusing your friendships with fun and laughter boosts the happiness and well-being of you all.

10. Invest time and effort in your friendships

Nurturing good friendships is like cultivating a beautiful garden – it takes time and effort but the rewards are worth it.

People with lots of friends are those who make time for friendships alongside other commitments, no matter how busy they are.

From a time perspective, friendship is a choice. If you want more friends, commit to investing more time and energy into finding and nurturing new connections.

Life often leads us down different paths from our friends but less time together or living further away doesn't have to end friendships. If you share a deep bond with someone, and you both want to remain friends, this is possible. Discuss with your friend how you both can navigate this new chapter together. By making a conscious effort to stay connected through regular phone calls, online chats, letters, or visits, you can preserve a sense of closeness and continuity in your friendship.

Key points

- Focus on what you can control and influence and embody being the friend you want others to be.

- Who you show up as influences the friendships you will experience. If you want to attract good friends, be one yourself.

- There are many ways to be a good friend. Everything I've shared here will enhance your friendships.

- Here's to you cultivating many invaluable friendships that will bring joy to your life for years to come.

Activity: Reflect on what you're taking away from this chapter in your journal.

Part Two
Seven Steps to Nourishing Friendships

Nourishing Friendships Workbook
Many of the following chapters have supporting practical exercises in my
Nourishing Friendships Workbook. This is available as a paperback on
Amazon or through my website: alisoun.com/friends

Chapter 8
Seven Steps to Making Nourishing Friends

Friendship complexities: a new phenomenon

There never used to be the need to seek out friends when we lived and worked in the same tight communities all through our lives. There was a limited pool of people who could become friends and we could get the support we needed from our community.

But in the modern world, people travel more for work, move house more frequently, and change jobs several times in a lifetime. This means we meet more people and often have less time to nurture friendships.

The increased popularity of online activities and working from home since the COVID-19 pandemic might have either reduced or increased opportunities to make friends, depending on your circumstances.

We can no longer rely on friendships evolving from the people we meet in day-to-day activities. We're also living longer, and with a broader range of activities available to us, we have a more varied range of friendship needs than our ancestors.

Knowing how to make the right friends is a new phenomenon and a skill set. If you're lucky, you'll have learned how to do this from life experience. But that's not the case for many people. That's why so many adults are struggling with friendships and, like you, are searching for tips on how to do this better.

In this chapter, I share seven steps to making nourishing friends. We will delve deeper into each of these in the following chapters.

How do you make friends as an adult?

Most people start by thinking about where to meet new people. This can work fine, and of course, you can meet wonderful friends by chance. However, I invite you to be more intentional about your friendship choices. When you first explore steps 1 to 4 below, you will increase the feasibility of meeting people who could become long-term friends.

By following all seven simple steps, in the order they are presented, you'll find it easier to find and enjoy friendships with the right people. You'll also be less likely to feel so alone or to experience conflict, drama, or bullying. The first four steps relate to your inner world (your beliefs, needs, values, and desires). Then the last three relate to the practical ways to meet people and nurture relationships.

Step 1 – Connect to your why

You're more likely to develop lasting friendships when the people you choose to spend time with align with your values, needs, goals, and approach to life.

This requires becoming more consciously aware of *why* you want more friends: how you hope new friends will change your life, what you'd love to do with them, and what truly matters to you. For instance, are you looking for local friends to go out with regularly or friends to go on holiday with (so they don't necessarily need to live nearby)?

Being clear about your reasons for wanting more friends will help you to be more focused and selective in prioritising relationships with people who have the greatest potential to become good friends. You will explore this in the next chapter.

Step 2 – Embrace a positive friendship mindset

Overcome negative thoughts, emotional blocks, and social anxiety, so that you feel more confident about finding friends who nourish your soul.

Most people have some doubts, fears, or insecurities about themselves, and that is human nature. However, if these feelings hinder your efforts to make friends, it's time to let them go.

Regardless of your age or past friendship experiences, it's possible to overcome any mindset blocks and emotional triggers you may have – even if you don't yet know how. Undoubtedly, it's not always easy but it is possible for most people. Most importantly, you deserve to be happy and surrounded by life-enriching friends. Find out how to embrace a good friendship mindset in Chapter 10.

Step 3 – Make friends with yourself

It's important to get clarity on who you really are. Friendships you nurture align with who you truly are and the type of friendships you want to experience in the future.

Many people, however, feel disconnected from their true self, the authentic person they were born to be. They've often lost sight of who they are, have neglected their passions, or no longer know what brings them joy.

Sometimes the friends we've had in the past no longer reflect who we are or want to become. This is especially true when you change direction, take up new hobbies, move somewhere new, or transition into a new stage of life.

If you want to make good friends who will accompany you on the next stage of your journey, connect with the essence of who you are now and the friends you want to meet. You'll discover how to do this in Chapter 11.

Step 4 – Define your ideal friends' qualities

To increase the likelihood of enjoying harmonious, nourishing friendships, identify all the qualities (e.g. values, mindset, emotional resilience, passions, skills, and behaviours) of people you'd like in your life – before you reach out to make friends.

Making conscious decisions about this effectively creates a set of filters that makes it easier to identify and focus on nurturing friendships with people who are most likely to love you, respect you, and value your friendship as much as you do theirs. That's why you'll explore and define your own criteria for what makes a good, nourishing friend to you in Chapter 12.

Step 5 – Review existing contacts

Once you've got clear on the type of friends you want, and why, the next focus is to find friends – and it isn't solely about meeting new people. You may already have people in your extended social circle who could become good friends if you were to invest time in getting to know them better. Find out more in Chapter 13.

Step 6 – Make new friends

If you feel you don't know enough people who could be the type of friend you're looking for, now's the time to consider where you could go to meet new like-minded people. I share tips for where to go and what to say when you meet people for the first time in Chapter 14.

Step 7 – Nurture nourishing friendships

Neglecting to nurture relationships is one of the main reasons many people lack friends. So, investing time and energy into nurturing and maintaining relationships is critical if you want more good friends. This involves adopting a proactive approach by initiating regular catch-ups, embracing new friendship habits, and creating energising friendship rituals. When you do this, your friendships will blossom more easily, and you're more likely to feel a sense of love, connection, and belonging. You'll find out how to do this in Chapter 15.

Key points

- Making friends is a skill set. The best way to make friends depends on your needs, values, desires, skills, behaviours, and people you already know.

- Following all seven steps will help you find and attract good friends to go out with and have fun with, and also friends who will offer mutual love and support.

- You may already know people, e.g. on your mobile contact list or on social media, who could be good friends if you were to nurture your relationship with them.

- Making friends involves taking time to get to know yourself and the type of people you want – and don't want – as friends.

- You're more likely to make good friends when you're selective about the places you go to meet people and who you nurture relationships with.

- You deserve to be surrounded by good friends who love you as much as you do them. But whether that happens depends on what you do next.

Chapter 9
Step 1 – Connect to Your Why

Connect to what really matters so you can enjoy friendships aligned with what's most important to you

Exploring how friendships could enrich your life enables you to make better-informed friendship choices, including where to find the right people and who to prioritise.

An inner journey of self-discovery

This involves connecting to your heart and what's important to you. To do this, ask yourself the following questions:

- **Why specifically do I want more friends?** – getting clear on why you want friends will help you to be more specific about the type of friends you're looking for, and where to meet them. For example, you may be lonely and want local friends you can go out with and talk to regularly.

- **What kind of friends do I want?** – you'll be exploring this more in Chapter 11, although it's important to jot down any initial thoughts you have now, too.

- **What do I want to do with friends in the future?** – think about what you'd love to be doing in the future, e.g. maybe you'd love to travel more but none of your existing friends share this passion (or can't find the time or money to join you), and so you're looking for friends to go on holiday with. The same could apply to hobbies you want to take up or activities on your bucket list. Or you may be looking for friends to share particular experiences with, e.g. concerts, theatre, or films.

- **When do people need to be available?** – we all have different priorities and commitments. You may meet someone who could be a great friend, but they are not available at the same time of day or week as you. If you have any time restraints, be conscious of these so that you can nurture friendships with people who are available at the same time as you.

～

I have friends I'd love to see but our schedules don't match. One such friend, Helen, I met while doing voluntary work in Poland over 30 years ago. We'd kept in touch with Christmas card messages and occasionally via social media, but we hadn't seen each other since the 1990s. Then she joined one of my online events and we were both keen to rekindle our friendship via Zoom as she lives several hours away. But she's a single parent and teacher and is only available late evenings. Unfortunately, I had chronic fatigue, and rarely made it to evenings. So, we spent around two months trying to find a time to talk but didn't manage – until recently. I was visiting relatives near where she lives and got in touch to see if she fancied meeting up. She did, and we had a fantastic afternoon together. I can't wait for us to see each other again!

～

You never know when it's the right time for people to become part of your life again. Sometimes it's not when you first hope. But if you're patient and keep in touch, you never know what can happen.

- **How do I want to feel around friends?** – the way people make you feel is a strong indication of whether a relationship is good for you or not. People don't set out to make friends with people who will hurt or abuse them. Yet, plenty of people find themselves in unhealthy friendships – often because they see the best in people, want to help them, or don't feel worthy of being friends with certain people. Getting clear on how you want to feel around people, and being more consciously aware of this, could help you avoid getting into the wrong friendships.

- **How do I hope friends will enhance my life?** – consider the positive impact more good friends could have on your life, and reflect on the benefits to others too. For example, if you are in a romantic relationship, you may want friends you go out with yourself and others you can socialise with as a couple.

- **What unmet needs do I have?** – friends can help you to get your needs met, e.g. to feel a deeper sense of connection, meaning, or belonging. Or to help you get through a new or challenging situation such as becoming a parent for the first time, becoming involuntarily childless, going through menopause, suffering from chronic illness, losing your job, or the loss of a loved one.

~

One of the most common things I hear retired women say is that they want friends to go on holiday with or to enjoy retirement adventures with. Typically, these are people with time on their hands but who don't have many friends in a similar position. By getting clear on this need and desire you can then take action to find people to go away with. If this is you, it's worth first having conversations with people you know, and exploring the many online groups and holidays where you can join an organised group.

~

- **What is important to me (my values)?** – having shared values is a strong foundation for any relationship. I don't just mean the values you say you have, but also the way you demonstrate your values through your actions. For instance, if you value peace over war, how do you contribute to a sense of loving peace at home, in relationships, or by attending peace demonstrations? How often do you feel angry or get caught up in an argument (and therefore are not living this value fully)? What values do you demonstrate through your behaviours?

- **What friendships are no longer working for me?** – we can gain great insights about good friendships by considering why some friendships are no longer working or have broken down. Reflecting on these can highlight negative behaviours we want to avoid in the future and mistakes we may have made. First, list friendships that have ended or are not working. Then for each, ask yourself, Why? Also, ask yourself, What part did I play in this friendship changing or ending?

Key points

- Getting clarity on why you want more friends is an invaluable exercise to do before looking for new friends.

- Doing this will help you make smarter friendship choices.

Activity: Find somewhere quiet and comfortable and answer the above questions in a journal or your Nourishing Friendships Workbook.

Chapter 10
Step 2 – Embrace a Positive Friendship Mindset

Break free from self-sabotaging beliefs and emotional blocks so you find it easier to make friends

When you think of the future, how confident are you that you'll have good friends who love and appreciate you as you do them?

It's natural to have doubts about meeting new people and making friends. At their best, these insecurities show up as nerves you choose to push through and carry on, regardless.

However, sometimes doubts, worries, fears, or anxieties are so intense they can hold you back from doing what it takes to make friends. The good news is that in the same way you've learned all your current beliefs and emotional triggers, you can learn to change what's not working – so you can feel more confident about making friends.

In this chapter, you will explore limiting beliefs and emotional blocks you have around friendship so that you can let these go and find it easier to make new friends.

The power of your thoughts

Everything you think, feel, and do influences the people and opportunities you attract.

Your thoughts shape your reality

The diagram above is the model I discuss in my book *Heartatude, The 9 Principles of Heart-Centered Success*[1]. It depicts how your thoughts and feelings influence what you do, how you do it, and in this context, the friends you subsequently attract. You attract good friends when all four factors are aligned:

- The **sun** – represents **what's important to you**, as we covered in the last chapter.

- The **head** – represents **your thoughts**, including beliefs, skills, and knowledge. These all influence how you feel. This chapter explores some beliefs that impact your friendships.

- The **heart** – represents **your feelings**. These influence what you do and how you do it, including whether you take action, e.g. to make more friends.

---

1. Alisoun Mackenzie, *Heartatude, The 9 Principles of Heart-Centered Success,* 2015.

- The **person** – represents **your actions and habits.** These in turn influence the results you get, and how others perceive you, e.g. whether people you meet want to be friends with you.

By aligning your thoughts, feelings, and actions with what's important to you, you'll make more friends.

If you have few good friends, this indicates a misalignment. This might be not being sure how to make friends, or doubts, insecurities, or bad habits. Your unconscious beliefs and emotional triggers, usually win the day.

Explore what's on the other side of your comfort zone

I take great inspiration from something I heard the adventurer Bear Grylls say a few years ago during a radio interview, that life is more exciting on the other side of your comfort zone.

Imagine believing this to be true as you embark upon this journey of making more friends. Feeling confident and at ease going to new places... meeting new interesting people... speaking to people for the first time... enjoying conversations that flow naturally... inviting people you like out... saying 'no' when you don't want to see people again... saying 'yes' more to the things you'd love to do...

- How would that feel?
- What would you do differently?
- How much better could your experience of friendships be?

I invite you to explore what's on the other side of your comfort zone and be open to the possibilities that could unfold.

Change your thoughts to change your future

- Are you nervous about speaking to new people or going out?
- Are you ever unsure of what to say when you meet people?
- Do you avoid inviting people out in case they say 'no'?

Fortunately, if any of your existing thoughts about making friends are holding you back, you can change them, so that you can overcome resistance and feel more confident. How do you do this? That depends upon how ingrained your thoughts and beliefs are. For some people, reading different perspectives, learning new skills – e.g. how to make friends, or using simple techniques such as affirmations (see below) – is a good starting point.

However, if you have deep-rooted beliefs or trauma-based emotional triggers, you might need to use techniques that work more deeply at an unconscious level, such as NLP (neurolinguistic programming), hypnotherapy, EFT (tapping), kinesiology, or Theta Healing. It's often best to do this with the support of an experienced therapist.

Affirmations

One way to change your mindset so that you find it easier to make friends is to reframe limiting beliefs into positive statements, known as affirmations. Affirmations work at a conscious level, so you need to say them repeatedly, several times a day, for at least fourteen days, to change how you think or feel. They are most effective when said in the present tense, although if this feels too much of a stretch, you could start them with, 'I'm open to the possibility I...' or 'I can...' Here are some examples:

Old negative belief: 'I'm scared of rejection.'

If you believe this to be true, you're more likely to feel stress, anxiety, or resistance which stops you from going out, inviting people to meet up, or saying 'yes' to good opportunities. You're also more likely to come across to others as doubtful and lacking in confidence.

New belief: 'The more I ask people out, the more friends I'll have.'

When you believe this to be true, you're likely to have more friends. Of course, some people will say 'no', but by asking more people out, you'll meet more people who will say 'yes'. I don't know anyone who likes rejection, but confident people accept that fears and rejection accompany them through life yet don't let that hold them back. When you do this, you'll also appear more confident and attract more confident people. And the more you do this, the easier it becomes.

What beliefs do you have about friendships?

The first step is to become more consciously aware of thoughts you have that could be holding you back from making good friends. Below are limiting friendship beliefs which clients have shared with me, together with alternative perspectives and empowering affirmations:

- **'People don't like me'** – everyone has people who don't like them in the same way you probably don't like everyone. Focus on meeting like-minded people and assume they will like you. Empowering belief: **'Like-minded people will like me.'**

- **'Friends are hard work'** – friendships are usually only hard work if you pick the wrong friends, don't set boundaries, or others find your views or behaviours challenging. Empowering belief: **'I have good, easy friendships.'**

- **'I'm not good enough'** – everyone deserves to have good friends. Consider what you can contribute to friendships. Empowering belief: **'I have lots to contribute to friendships.'**

- **'I don't have many friends'** – even if this is true now, it doesn't have to stay this way. Empowering belief: **'I'm having fun making new friends.'**

- **'I don't know where to meet people'** – there are plenty of places to make new friends. Empowering belief: **'I'm exploring new places and meeting like-minded people.'**

- **'I feel awkward speaking to people I don't know'** – this is a skill you can learn that becomes easier with practice. Empowering belief: **'I'm getting better at asking questions and speaking to people.'**

- **'I sometimes make friends, but they don't last'** – most friendships are temporary. Where you've lost friends in the past, ask yourself, 'What part did I play in the friendship ending?'

Also consider what you could do differently in the future. Empowering belief: **'I'm good at maintaining friendships with people I like.'**

- **'I'm scared of rejection/that people will say 'no''** – this is a common fear and yet 'no' is part of life. It might be to do with their circumstances, not because they don't like you. Confident people embrace their fears and ask people out. Empowering belief: **'The more I ask people out, the more friends I will have.'**

- **'People never ask me out'** – waiting to be asked out means you could be letting good friends and opportunities pass you by. You are the only person who can create the best opportunities for you. Empowering belief: **'I have more friends because I ask people out.'**

- **'Friends hurt me'** – no-one likes getting hurt. If you pick the right friends and believe in yourself, you're less likely to get hurt. Sometimes it's also worth accepting that everyone makes mistakes. Empowering belief: **'I can find kind, loving friends.'**

- **'I'm too old to make new friends'** – you're never too old to make new friends. Empowering belief: **'There are lots of people looking for friends like me.'**

- **'I don't know what to say to people'** – you don't need many questions to get a conversation going, as you'll learn later in this book. Empowering belief: **'I have a few questions I can ask when I first meet people.'**

What doubts do you have that hold you back from making friends?

Unsure what's holding you back?

The PAW process is a simple affirmation model that categorises all doubts and limiting beliefs into three areas: Possibility, Ability, and Worthiness.

1. Possibility

Before you do something, you first have to believe it's possible. Only once you believe it's possible for others can you believe it could be possible for you too. If you want good friends, you first need to believe people can enjoy great friendships. Then it's a case of learning to believe it's possible for you too.

Do you believe it's possible to have good friends? If not, write an affirmation that starts with 'It's possible for me...', e.g. it's possible for me to make good friends...

2. Ability

Once you believe something is possible, the next level of doubt is around ability. If you ever say 'I can't' that's feedback you doubt your ability and it's time to reframe your beliefs. You will learn the basics of how to make good friends in this book including:

- How to turn contacts and acquaintances into close friends.
- Where to find new friends.
- What to say when you meet people and when you want to ask people out.
- How to set boundaries and say 'no' without feeling guilty.
- How to be a good friend.
- How to end a friendship.
- How to resolve conflicts with friends.
- Red flags to watch for so you avoid unhealthy friendships.
- How to cope better when friendships end.
- How to rekindle friendships.

All these topics are covered in this book. If you knew all of this, do you think you'd find it easier to make friends?

To cultivate a positive friendship mindset, craft affirmations that start with 'I can / I can learn / I have the ability to...', e.g. I can physically ask people out. Repeat these several times a day and every time you feel nervous or feel you can't.

~

'I used to be scared to ask people out, but Alisoun helped me see things differently. I always thought if someone said 'no', it meant they didn't like me. I didn't think there could be other reasons. It took time, but I now feel more confident asking people to meet up again. I have two new friends because I didn't wait to be asked out. One friend I meet regularly for a chat and another I'm planning a holiday with.' Alena

~

3. Worthiness

Once you believe something is possible and that you can do something (or learn how to do it), the third level of doubt is around worthiness. This is often the biggest mindset and emotional block.

Some attendees at my events originally felt that they had nothing to offer friends. They could accept the concepts of possibility and ability but they were unsure what they could contribute to friendships. They thought they had nothing to offer. Thankfully, it only took a few minutes of coaching for them to see they had lots they could offer others, e.g. time, company to do things, someone to speak to, a kind heart, being a good listener, having a good sense of humour, being helpful, loyal, and trustworthy, etc. By simply focusing on what they could contribute, they began to feel more deserving and confident about making new friends.

Do you feel you deserve to be surrounded by good friends who will support and cherish you as much as you do them? If not, complete this affirmation, 'I deserve to...', e.g. I deserve to be surrounded by good friends.

Or use a cover-all-bases affirmation: 'It's possible, I can do it, I deserve it!'

Developing a new mindset and habits takes practice

Consider when you learned to walk. Most people around you were walking around and so you believed it would be possible for you. While you didn't have the strength in your body to walk initially, you gave it a shot as you believed it was possible. You got up and fell down. Got up and fell down. You repeated this again and again until you developed the strength and the skills to walk.

Just imagine what you could achieve if you applied that same level of determination that you applied to learning to walk, to make good friends. I'm sure you'd start to see better results.

Key points

- Your mindset, confidence, emotional triggers, and habits all influence the friendships you make.

- Feeding negative beliefs or emotional triggers with your time and attention will sabotage future friendships.

- In the same way you have learned everything else you know now, you can learn to change your mindset – so you can feel more confident and find it easier to make friends.

- If in doubt, repeat or adapt the following affirmation or mantra: 'It's possible to make friends. I can do this. I deserve lots of good friends.'

Activity: How could you choose to think or feel differently?

Chapter 11
Step 3 – Make Friends With Yourself

Get clear on who you are and what you want so that your friendships reflect this

One of the reasons we fall in and out of friendships is that we all change. Whether through personal choice or differing life experiences, there are many reasons why friends come and go.

Many of us have also spent years conforming to others' expectations rather than having the confidence or privilege to live a truly authentic life – where you feel free, accepted, and loved as the unique person you were born to be.

Make friends with yourself first

- Have you ever lost sight of who you are?
- Are you fed up with life and eager for change?
- Are you going through a life transition or wondering what's next?

If you've answered yes to any of these questions, some of your friendships may not be close friends in the future. This doesn't mean you need to let those friendships go – it's healthy to have a range of friends. However, making friends with people who share your new passions and interests fulfils other needs. That's why it's important to consider who you are and what you want, so that you can choose friends who will enrich the next stage of your life.

It's also worth reflecting on the kind of friend you are, what you've got to contribute to friendships, and the extent to which you are the friend you want others to be. That's what you'll explore in this chapter.

Who am I?

Most of your insights will come from inner reflection. Depending on how happy you are with your life and the scope of your commitments and interests, this will either be a straightforward task or the catalyst for a deeper, longer-term journey of personal discovery. Either way, answering the following questions will help you make good friends in the future.

Sometimes, you meet someone who understands a part of you better than you know yourself. I have one such friend: a kind, loving, and wise soul who I adore. Our conversations are always thought-provoking and inspiring, often sprinkled with laughter too. As a coach, she regularly challenges me in ways other friends don't, to dig deeper and become a better version of myself. Her intuitive wisdom and spiritual insights are invariably right. Not only that, most of my local friends can be traced back to our friendship. I'm in awe and ooze gratitude for this amazing soul I'm privileged to call my friend.

How do I describe myself?

We often describe ourselves as what we do, or how we feel, rather than who we are. Of course, you have several roles in life that feed your sense of identity, but they don't define you. Your past, health, skills, personality, values, passions, energy, mindset, approach to life, and dreams for the future are also all important.

What are my best qualities?

Think about what you know you're good at. These could be your skills or mindset, how you cope with life, or how you make people feel. Remember any compliments and words of thanks which people have said about you.

How easy do I find it to trust people?

Trust is essential for all friendships. If you find it hard to trust people or it takes you a long time, others may feel they can't connect with you at a level they need to be close friends. Conversely, if you trust people too much or too quickly, you could be taken advantage of. We all also have different thresholds for what constitutes a breach of trust. The key is to have a good self-awareness of your relationship to trust, and how this could impact your friendships.

What do I love doing?

This includes all activities you love doing now and those you enjoyed in the past. Think about hobbies, interests, and activities, even those you have done once or twice. What did you love doing when you were younger? What used to bring you joy?

What do I want to do in the future?

The decisions you make now influence what you'll experience in the future. Take a moment to dream, and imagine all the things you'd love to do. What's on your bucket list? What would you like to learn or try? Consider the things you enjoy reading about, watching on TV, and films or videos you consume.

What impact do I want to have in the world?

At the end of the day, all that really matters is your impact, how you've made others feel and the difference you've made. What would make you feel proud when you look back on your life? What would you love people to say about you, your life, or legacy?

To what extent do I love myself?

Good friends can help reduce feelings of loneliness, but they don't fix everything. It's still possible to feel lonely in relationships, especially if you experienced neglect or trauma, or you don't like yourself.

Self-love isn't arrogance. It's about learning to love yourself as you would the baby version of yourself. Being kind and loving towards yourself is at the heart of self-love – what you think about yourself and how you treat your body, mind, and soul.

Of course, learning to like or love yourself is an extremely complex topic. But wherever you are now is the perfect starting point and there is no need to feel you need to 'fix' yourself before making friends. By choosing to embark upon a healing journey of personal growth and discovery, you may meet people who could become friends.

That said, if you are feeling any extreme feelings of self-hate, loathing, or helplessness, please seek professional support now to help you feel better about yourself.

～

I remember the first time someone suggested it was good to love myself. I thought they were mad. Such a statement sounded untrue, arrogant, and certainly not something ingrained in the Scottish psyche. They asked me: if you don't love yourself, why would anyone else love you? That question floored me.

I spent years unpacking the self-doubt and criticism I'd learned to believe about myself since childhood. Gradually I started feeling much better about myself and no longer wanted to be around people who regularly criticised me or put me down. I started gravitating more towards people who also believed in themselves and others.

～

What makes me a good friend?

Remember, who you show up as influences the type of friends you have. I shared tips on how to be a good nourishing friend in Chapters 6 and 7. Review these, and take a few moments to jot down what you think makes you a good friend. Think about your personal values, qualities, and what you've got to offer friends – e.g. time – and ways you like to connect with and support friends.

How do I demonstrate I care?

Now it's time to consider your preferred ways of showing friends you are thinking of them, love and appreciate them. I shared examples of how to demonstrate that you care in Chapter 7. Refer to this list and consider all the different ways a friend would know you are thinking of them, care for them, and appreciate the part they play in your life.

Here is an example of what one of my best friends did for me. On my way to bed one night, I went to lock up my front door, only to find a surprise in my front porch: a gift bag and a card. I picked it up with curiosity. It wasn't my birthday. Who would leave me a gift for no reason? I locked the door, and went through to my kitchen, where I opened the bag. Inside was a beautiful statement mug from one of my friends with the following words on it: 'I'm a joy bringer'. But I still didn't know who it was from. Until I opened the card. My friend had written a beautiful message sharing how much she valued our friendship and how I brought joy into her life. The mug and her words were two of the most precious gifts I've ever received because she's someone I love and cherish, too. A couple of years later I still use that mug most days I'm at home. This is just one of the many ways this friend goes out of her way to show me she cares.

What restrictions do I have (that I can't change)?

Making nourishing friends can be a wonderful experience, yet it also takes time and effort.

While on this journey, you're likely to meet people you'd love to be friends with, but other factors might limit this possibility. These could be existing relationships and hobbies, family commitments, work obligations, health conditions, financial restraints, or where you live.

Sometimes restrictions are genuine reasons that we're not a good fit with people in the way we'd like. For example, if you work full-time or travel a lot, you may only be available at weekends. Or the opposite could be true, meaning you're only available to make friends with people who are also available during the day.

Limitations are reasons why your ability to make friends is restricted but watch to make sure that they don't become excuses. This happens when you give reasons too much power and don't explore how you could make friends despite limitations.

When I was ill with chronic fatigue and mainly housebound, I could have stepped back from my friendships. But my friends, and particularly those closest to me, are really important to me. And so, while I couldn't physically go out and meet people, I had lots of Zoom calls, to maintain friendships and my sanity! Was this ideal? No. But it made getting through a challenging time easier. While I only had the energy to do this with my closest friends, I also sent occasional emails or messages to other good friends.

Likewise, if you're struggling financially, this may limit what you can do. But it is still possible to have great friends despite this. It's about the choices you make, in terms of who you seek to be friends with and the activities you decide to do. For example, you could go for a walk, picnic, or round to each other's homes for a cuppa or meal rather than doing more expensive activities. Start by considering what you do yourself already, e.g. eating, drinking, reading, watching films. Then make arrangements to do these with others.

Be mindful of the story you share with others

The 'story' you tell others about yourself, especially when you first meet them, will influence their perceptions of you, and the type of friend you could be to them. Ideally, you want to share honest stories that project your desired impression of you. Follow this process to craft stories aligned with your ideal friends:

1. If I were to meet you for the first time, what would you tell me about yourself?
2. Ask yourself, how do I want new people to perceive me?
3. Review your first answer, through the filters of how you want others to perceive you. Would your first answer give people a glimpse of the person you want to be known as? If yes, that's great. However, if the story doesn't match the experiences you want to have with friends in the future, rewrite it – so it reflects what it would be better to share.

I share more about what to say to people when you first meet them in Chapter 14.

Be kind to yourself when making friends

In the last chapter I discussed the importance of embracing a positive friendship mindset. Yet, many people forget to be kind to themselves when making friends. To do this, ask yourself, 'What makes me a good friend?' and 'What would make it easier for me to make friends?' You could:

- Remind yourself what you have to contribute as a friend.
- Ask people to accompany you to events so you feel more at ease and confident.
- Identify and reframe doubts that hold you back.
- Say 'yes' to things you really want to do, and say 'no' when you don't feel good about the prospect of what's being suggested – unless you'd love to but have doubts, in which case it would be good to push yourself out of your comfort zone.

- Accept everyone makes mistakes – you and others.
- Repeat the mantra: I always do the best I can.
- Remember when someone says 'no', it doesn't mean they don't like you.
- Take time to get to know and like yourself.
- Do activities that make you feel good naturally, e.g. going for a walk, massage, or having a bath.

Key points

- Making friends with yourself will help you enjoy the future you yearn for – with the type of friends you want to meet.

- At the heart of making friends with yourself is tapping into what you enjoy and want to do in the future, while also being confident about what makes you a good friend.

Activity: Reflect on the questions in this chapter, so you have a greater awareness of who you are and what you want to share and do with friends in the future.

Chapter 12
Step 4 – Define Your Ideal Friendship Qualities

Get clarity on the type of friends you want so your friendships are easy and uplifting

∾

I was scared, nervous, and full of dread as I considered dating after the end of my first marriage. I'd learned from past mistakes and was determined to avoid the same red flags in future relationships. To do this I knew I needed to be more intentional about the type of people I wanted to let into my life. And so I sat at my kitchen table, writing down what was important to me and the values, qualities, behaviours, and attributes I was seeking in my ideal partner... as well as all the things I didn't want. This list became invaluable when choosing who to date, and it helped me meet a wonderful guy who is now my husband.

∾

The same intentional approach can be applied to making friends. By being clear about the qualities you want in your friendships, you will find it easier to surround yourself with friends who bring out the best in you, energise you, and make you feel loved and supported.

Benefits of identifying your ideal friendship qualities

Knowing your ideal friendship qualities helps you to make smarter friendship choices including:

- The type of people you want to spend time with.
- Where to go to meet people.
- Relationships to nurture versus let go.
- Values and behaviours that are deal breakers.
- Setting boundaries and managing relationships better.

What are your ideal friendship qualities?

Your ideal friendship qualities are positive attributes you look for in your friends. These include:

- **Values** – what's important to you in life, relationships, friendships, etc.

- **Interests** – the activities you enjoy or would like to learn.

- **Personality traits** – the essence of who someone is and the behaviours they display naturally and consistently.

- **Behaviours** – what people do and how they do it. In this context, particularly how they treat you and others.

- **Mindset** – the beliefs people have about themselves, others, and the world around them.

- **Skills** – the skills you'd like your ideal friends to have, e.g. being a good listener and communicator, calm, assertive, a problem solver, a team player, and an ability to make you feel good.

You may find it helpful to review the attributes I shared in Chapters 6 and 7. But remember, these are only my ideas. You may have different ones. The purpose of this chapter is to help you refine these.

Who do you want to be friends with?

A helpful way to get more clarity is to consider the positive values, qualities, and behaviours of existing friends. Think of three to five good friends – past, present, or imaginary. For each friendship, ask yourself:

- What do I like about this person?
- What do I like and appreciate about the friendship we have?
- How do they treat me?
- What's missing in the friendship?
- What could be better about the friendship?
- How do they make me feel?

If you don't have many friends or want to focus on creating new friendships, think about someone you'd like to be friends with or characters you admire from dramas, films, or books.

Qualities people come up with at my events include: fun, positive, optimistic, proactive, similar interests, a sense of humour, value time with friends and family, fascinating, interesting, open-minded, honest, trustworthy, kind, loving, compassionate, forgiving, high sense of integrity, curious, adventurous, make a difference, environmentally friendly, helpful, thoughtful, solutions focused, action takers, activists, and people who take a stand for what's important to them.

Who do you NOT want to be friends with?

It is not good for you to be in unhealthy relationships, e.g. with people who consistently put you down, hurt, or abuse you. So, it's also important to note down the values, behaviours, interests, and qualities of people you want to stay away from; the deal breakers of any potential friendship. To do this, think of people you don't like, you've had a clash with, or a friendship that has gone wrong. Then ask yourself:

- What behaviours did I not like?
- How did they treat me?
- How did they make me feel?
- What type of people do I want to stay away from?

Creating a list of negative attributes highlights red flags – so you can avoid and get out of friendships that are not good for you, sooner rather than later. Is this way mean, nasty or manipulative? No. You deserve to be surrounded by people who make you feel good. You don't deserve to be treated badly. It's only natural that you won't like everyone, and not everyone will like you. Having personal preferences is a natural fact of life.

Embracing diversity when making friends

Robin Dunbar[1] identified the following seven pillars of friendship:

1. Speaking the same language.
2. Growing up in the same location.
3. Having similar educational and career experiences.
4. Enjoying the same interests and hobbies.
5. Having the same world view.
6. Sharing the same sense of humour.
7. Having the same musical tastes.

He found that these key factors influence how much time you're likely to be prepared to invest in a relationship with someone. The more you have in common with them, the more likely you gravitate towards them.

I find it helpful to understand these natural affiliations, but I also feel that if you limit your friendships only to being with those who are similar to you, you could stifle your growth and exclude people who could enrich your life. Sometimes the best friendships are with people who are different from us.

I therefore also suggest connecting with kind people who offer new perspectives. Ways to do this include being open to building friendships with kind, open-minded people from different backgrounds, people who have a different point of view, or who had very different life experiences. Plus, people of all capabilities, ages, genders, neurodiversity, sexual orientations, and ethnic origins. Rather than focusing on what makes you

---

1. A renowned anthropologist, evolutionary psychologist, and professor at Oxford University.

different, focus on any similarities and how you could embrace and learn from them.

Fortunately, there is a growing understanding of neurodiversity which acknowledges that we are all wired differently. This influences our behavioural traits. In the past, many people viewed differences as disorders. But this 'othering' mindset leads to unfair judgments and treatment of those who are considered outside the 'norm'. However, people who think differently are often fascinating, exceptionally talented, and could prove to be good friends.

As a starting point, be mindful of any potential judgements you make about people when you meet them. Rather than feeding any prejudices and too quickly writing off people who are different to you, be open to getting to know them as a potential friend.

Who else could enrich my life?

The people you surround yourself with greatly influence your experience of life. Want to learn something new? Surround yourself with people further down the road than you, and you'll find it easier to make this shift. Also, consider the different ways you could immerse yourself in this.

If you're going through a life transition or challenging situation, consider whether it would be beneficial for you to connect and get support from people experiencing something similar. It's also often easier to make friends and changes in life with the support of an experienced life coach.

Consolidate your list of ideal friendship qualities

Now it's time to consolidate and refine your list. Take all your answers and create one list of ideal friendship qualities split into:

- **Critical qualities** – essential qualities you look for in all friendships.

- **Optional qualities** – desirable qualities for some but not all friendships. Remember, no friend will satisfy all your needs. It's also natural for your selection criteria for new friendships to evolve as you change, grow, and age. It's also possible to love and appreciate long-term friends who don't share all the same qualities as you may look for in new friendships.

- **Deal breakers** – undesirable behaviours or values that clash with what's important to you and highlight a need for caution and firm boundaries.

∿

One of my optional qualities is that my friends are global citizens: people who care about global issues and take action to make a difference. I have some good friends from the past for whom this isn't important, and I love each one for being the friend they are in my life. However, this has become an important aspect for me over the last few years, and it is a quality I look for in new friendships.

∿

Now you have a list of your ideal friendship qualities, you'll be able to refer to this as you evaluate friendships and prioritise the type of friends you want to focus on making first.

To what extent are you one of your ideal friends?

You attract people who are like you, so to attract your ideal friends, you need to embody those qualities yourself when you're out and about. That's why it's worth considering how well you reflect the friend you hope to find in others.

First, review your ideal friendships qualities list and score yourself on a scale of 0-10 against each desired quality, with 10 being 100% true. Then reflect on any aspects of yourself that could be worth changing, developing, or refining. Whatever comes up for you, be kind to yourself and recognise who you are right now is fine. You're on a journey.

Key points

- When you clearly define the qualities you seek in friendships, you'll find it easier to make friends with people who will uplift you, energise you, and support you.

- This includes being clear on the type of friends you don't want.

- Embrace diversity too – to give you a broader perspective on the world and enjoy new experiences you'd otherwise miss out on.

- Consider the extent to which you are the type of friend you are looking for, to double-check whether there are ways you could show up as a better friend.

Activity: List all your ideal friendship qualities and split them into critical, optional, and red flags.

Chapter 13
Step 5 – Review Existing Contacts

It's easier to nurture good friendships with existing contacts

Most people who want to make new friends start by thinking about places to meet new people. Yet reviewing existing contacts can be a quicker way of finding people who could become good friends for the next stage of your life. Even if you think you don't have enough contacts for this, bear with me. There may be people lurking in your mobile phone or on social media who you've forgotten about.

Complete a friendship review

A friendship review is a process that enables you to:

- Acknowledge and prioritise good friends and relationships you want to invest in.

- Highlight people you'd like to get to know better – some people you already know who could become good friends for the next stage of your life.

- Identify people who are not good for you.

- Decide which friendships to nurture, maintain (with boundaries), or let go.

- Evaluate whether new people you meet align with your values, interests, and friendship needs.

Some people call this practice a friendship audit or detox but the terminology isn't really important; what matters is approaching this with clear intentions, and with love, kindness, and compassion – for yourself and others.

'Having built a significant network of friends, acquaintances, and work contacts during my 20-year corporate career, as I stepped away from that environment, I decided it was time to reflect on who I wanted to take with me. I knew I was unlikely to have the time or the mental and emotional energy to maintain all of those relationships. Many of them were simply not a relevant fit in my new life. So, I took the brave and difficult decision to carry out a relationship edit.

It was easy to identify relationships where I couldn't countenance the idea of no longer having these wonderful people in my life. The next phase was more difficult. I had acquaintances I'd known for many years, and we'd shared some joyful and difficult work experiences. But could I grow those relationships into lasting friendships? Around that time a close friend of mine shared the wise idea that friends are either 'for a reason, a season, or a lifetime'.

Sometimes the reason we connect falls away and the relationship with it. There is no harm in that. The point is to be continuously mindful about the extent to which love and values truly continue to be shared equally between you in whatever phase of life you are.' Morven

How to complete a friendship review

Follow this 5-step process to complete your friendship review and identify friends, potential friendships, and relationships to let go.

1. Identify your ideal friendship qualities

To increase the likelihood of enjoying nourishing, harmonious friendships, identify all the qualities of people you want in your life. This is what we explored in the last chapter.

2. Create a list of people you know

Go through ALL your contacts. Jot down existing friends and people you like – even if you've only met them briefly. Don't worry if you don't have many people on this list. I share where to meet new people in the next chapter. People to consider include:

- Existing friends, acquaintances, contacts.
- People on your Christmas card list.
- Mobile phone and email contacts.
- Social media friends and contacts – across all platforms.
- People you're in photos with.
- Friends from the past you could reconnect with.
- People you've interacted with recently – in person or online.
- Group contacts, e.g. people you know from clubs, community groups, or informal gatherings.
- Acquaintances you click with and would like to know better.
- People you've met at events and courses.

Use Post-it notes or small pieces of paper to make the next steps – with one name on each.

3. Refine your list

Now it's time to refine your list to mainly include good friends and potential friends. Review your list through the filters of your ideal friendship qualities: the type of friends you're looking for. Also, add friends you feel challenged by, yet still want to keep in your life, e.g. those you feel nostalgic about or who are in a mutual friendship group.

4. Complete your friends' matrix

Use this friendship matrix to prioritise the people on your list and decide
your next steps:

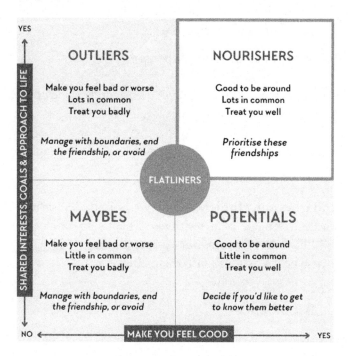

For each person, ask yourself the following questions:

- Does this person energise me and treat me well?
- Do I have much in common with this person?
- Do I value this friendship?
- Do I want to continue to be friends with this person?
- Could this person be a nourishing friend?

Place each person's name in the relevant quadrant of how they make you
feel. Then order the list in each quadrant. This is easier if you've put each
person's name on a small piece of paper and are using the blank matrix in
my Nourishing Friendships Workbook (available on Amazon).

Flat-liners – in the middle of the matrix are what one of my friends calls flat-liners, who are people who do nothing for you either way. You don't feel they're the type of person who'd become a friend.

It's natural for people to move from one quadrant to another through life, or as your relationship with them evolves.

5. Decide your next steps for each person:

- **The Nourishers** – prioritise these friends and decide how you want to nurture these friendships (see Chapter 15).

- **The Potentials** – if you want to get to know these people better, contact them.

- **The Maybes and Outliers** – either set boundaries with those you want to remain friends with (see Chapter 19) or let the friendship go (see Chapter 21). Avoid building close friendships with new people who fall into these categories.

Nostalgic friendships

These are often long-term friendships with people you have known for years and for whom you still feel a sense of love or affinity due to shared past experiences. It's natural for friendships to flow over the years from a close friendship to a cherished acquaintance, and sometimes back again. Where the friendship has changed to the extent that you no longer relate to one another, that's OK. If you no longer want to be friends, it may be time to let the friendship drift away naturally or to end it.

Friendship groups

Most people I've worked with mention people they don't click with in large friendship groups to the same extent. This is natural. As you complete your friendship matrix, consider each person in a group individually to decide the type of friendship you want – a group relationship only or a personal one, too.

~

'There's one person in my husband's group of friends that I don't like. There's nothing really wrong with them; we just have nothing in common except my husband, and I find them too needy. I used to think I had to be friends with them, but now I realise I don't. It's OK to just see them as part of the group. I can handle that. Finding out I don't need to be friends with everyone in a group was a huge relief, and liberating.' Joyce

~

Group dynamics are complex, yet the many benefits of being in a nourishing group of friends often make the need to carefully manage relationships worth the extra effort. Where you find someone in a group challenging, you may need to be assertive to stop negative behaviours towards you, e.g. by sharing your boundaries with them, or asking for others in the group to help navigate challenges between you. Other times, it may be about accepting that you don't need to be close friends, or managing your emotions so you feel better and cope better when in their company (see Chapter 17).

Key points

- A friendship review enables you to evaluate the current status of friendships, prioritise people you want to see, and identify gaps in your friendship circles. It can also help you find people you'd forgotten about who could become good friends.

- Culling challenging friendships isn't always the way to go and can be unnecessarily ruthless, particularly if your friend is going through a difficult time. In Chapter 22 I share factors to consider before ending friendships.

Activity: Complete a friendship review to identify friendships to nurture or let go.

Chapter 14
Step 6 – Make New Friends

Meet new people and make friends all through life

If you haven't identified many people to contact from your friendship review, or you've run out of people to contact, it's time to explore how to meet new like-minded people.

Ten ways to meet new people

1. Local clubs, classes, courses, and events

If you want more local friends to talk to or go out with, local activities where you can meet like-minded people are a good starting point. Prioritise the activities you're most excited about. To find local groups, do an online search, and check out notice boards in local shops, your library or health centre, or local Facebook groups.

2. National or international clubs, classes, and events

These can be good where the activity is more important to you than the desire to meet people locally. I love travelling and have found going to travel shows is a great way to meet like-minded people and hear about clubs/communities I can join. I've met lots of my current friends at personal development and business events around the world.

3. Volunteer for causes or projects that resonate with you

Volunteering can be an empowering way to feel you're making a difference, add meaning to your life, and meet new people with shared interests or values. You can volunteer regularly or on a one-off basis, depending on your needs, desires, and availability.

If you're looking for local friends, explore opportunities to volunteer in your immediate community. There are also opportunities to volunteer around the country (e.g. at festivals and sporting events) and overseas. [1]

Likewise, if you want to take a stand for something important to you, you could get involved in campaigns, fundraising events, or demonstrations. All are opportunities to meet and get to know new like-minded people.

4. Meet-up groups

Meetup.com is an online portal set up to encourage people with similar interests to meet in person. There are meet-up groups around the world for almost every interest you can think of. If I were to move somewhere new, checking out Meetup.com would be one of the first things I would do to meet people locally.

5. Online groups, apps, and communities

There are many online communities you could join, too, e.g. on Facebook, LinkedIn, or other online platforms. There are also communities and apps set up specifically to help you make friends. Do an online search to find the one(s) most suited to you.

6. Support groups on topics relevant to you

If you're struggling with anything in your life, there are likely to be support groups that can help and will introduce you to others in a similar position – either online or in person. I know that twenty years ago I would have welcomed a support group to help me come to terms with becoming involuntarily childless. It would also have been good to have had more childless friends to talk to and go out with.

---

1. If you have white privilege (you look white), be mindful of how to avoid being a white saviour when volunteering overseas. See a blog I've written on What's Wrong with Volunteering Overseas on my website here – https://alisoun.com/volunteering-overseas/

7. Set up a club or community group

If you can't find what you're looking for, consider setting up a club or group yourself. When you do this, you're not only likely to meet new people, by bringing others together, but you'll also bring joy to others. Setting up a group of like-minded people can also help you feel a greater sense of belonging – assuming you bring together the right people.

~

In 1994 I set up Scotland's first independent travel club. I'd been away for three years, and when I came back to Edinburgh I didn't know anyone else who enjoyed my new passion. By putting an advert in a local paper, I made lots of new like-minded friends, some of whom are still in my life over thirty years later. I feel it's a lot easier to do this now with social media platforms and groups. Likewise, running a business networking group was one of the best ways I've made wonderful long-term friendships.

~

8. Chat with people you meet in the course of a day

How often do you keep your head down or walk past people without engaging with them? When you're out and about and meeting people, there are plenty of opportunities to speak to them. Particularly where you meet people with a similar interest, e.g. while standing waiting to get into the class or queueing for a drink at an event.

~

A few years ago, I noticed some of my friends were much better at connecting with people in passing than me. They'd confidently speak to people at events, at a yoga class, or in the street. I remember thinking I'd love to be more like them. So, I decided to consciously step outside my comfort zone. I started putting my mobile away, looking up, and saying hello more. Sometimes, if it felt right, I'd ask a question to strike up a conversation. I now find it easier to connect and speak to people I'd like to get to know better. This, in turn, makes it easier to invite them for a cuppa and see where the relationship goes.

9. Organise events

Organising your own event and inviting people along is a great way to make new friends. This could be an informal event where people meet in a cafe, or a more formal paid event. If you want to meet new people, you share the event via a post in a 'safe' closed group on social media, reach out to people you know who may be interested, and ask people to share and bring other friends along.

~

'Even as an extrovert, I found it hard to make friends when I moved from a city I lived in for years, with a good support network, to a new more remote area. I really needed someone to invite me in and introduce me to their friends. Feeling socially isolated affected my confidence and being peri-menopausal didn't help. I needed friends more than ever but felt less able to reach out or make the effort to do new things. Now eight months in, I'm just starting to build relationships but it's taken much longer than I'd hoped. I've met two new local friends through a Facebook group for women over fifty, in which you can say where you are and who you want to meet. They were as pleased to meet me as I was to meet them. It's made all the difference.'
Marie Louise

~

10. Ask for introductions

Once you know what type of friends you want, share this with people you know and ask them to introduce you to people they know, who they think you'd get on with.

I recently saw someone post in a local Facebook group that she was new to the area and wanted to meet people. She shared a little about herself and asked if anyone would be interested in meeting up. By having the courage to share how she felt, she was inundated with people who offered to meet up with her.

∾

A close friend introduced me to someone she knew a few years ago. We instantly clicked, and that person is now one of my best friends. I'm so grateful to the friend who knew us both for introducing us to each other. She is not the only one of my friends who has done this. Many of my friends have been introduced to me by other friends. One special friend went out of her way to introduce me to many like-minded people when I moved into the area, even though I didn't know her that well then. This made a huge difference.

∾

Ten tips for making new friends

Applying much of what I've shared earlier in this book influences how successful you will be in making more friends. Below are my top tips to consider when you're out and about making new friends. I shared further tips in Chapter 3.

1. Have fun doing it your way

Choose ways to meet people that both connect you to your ideal friends and make you feel good. There are so many challenges we face in life and the world around us but it's much easier to cope when you can also have fun with friends. What if making friends could be fun?

2. Lean into the authentic person you were born to be

Life is too short to pretend to be someone you are not. Instead, get clear about who you are, what you love, what's important to you, what you can contribute to a friendship, and how you want to be perceived by others. This also includes embracing your personality traits, such as whether you're an introvert or extrovert, and how this influences your social preferences. For example, do you prefer to meet up with people one-to-one or as part of a group? Not sure who you are anymore or feel you're drifting aimlessly through life? Refer to Chapter 11 on Making Friends with Yourself.

3. Be mindful of others' perceptions of you

Everything you say and do, or choose not to, shapes how others perceive you. Some impressions form immediately upon meeting you. Others develop over time.

That's why it's important to ensure the stories you tell people about yourself align with the person you want to be perceived as in the future. This involves being intentional about the stories you share about yourself, as I discussed in Chapter 11.

For example, if you have interests and passions you'd love to do with friends, speak about these so that like-minded people know this. By mainly speaking about your past or the challenges you face, you're more likely to attract people who are stuck in the past or who face the same challenges. While, at the same time, you could lose out on potential friendships with people with similar interests or aspirations for the future – simply because you failed to mention these to them.

When meeting new people, also aim to strike a balance between being positive and showing a hint of vulnerability to foster connections. However, don't overshare. Expressing too much negativity or vulnerability too soon can make you appear needy, critical, or overly demanding. This can drive potential friends away.

Instead, focus on being friendly, upbeat, and supportive, gradually revealing more vulnerable aspects of yourself as the relationship develops. It's never about deceiving others but being mindful of what you share first.

4. Try out new activities

Make finding friends fun by seeing it as an opportunity to try things out you've always wanted to do, hobbies you used to enjoy, and activities you're curious about. Or those you're sceptical about or scared of. Learning new skills and trying out new activities is a great way to make good friends. What's on your bucket list?

~

I used to be so terrified of what lurks in the sea that I rarely went into it. I also didn't like putting my head underwater. However, after a few weeks of swimming lessons, I became a lot more confident in the water. That led me to try paddle boarding and I discovered I loved it – even when I fell in. During the Covid pandemic, I started swimming locally in the North Sea and made lots of new friends. Had I not done those swimming lessons all those years ago, I doubt I'd have these wonderful women in my life now.

~

Of course, going along to group classes rather than the one-to-one swimming lessons I did is a quicker way to make friends – especially if you go to regular classes or events with the same group of people.

5. Say 'YES' more often

Say 'yes' to opportunities where the only things holding you back are your fears or insecurities. I don't mean saying 'yes' to things you don't enjoy or are not good for you. Rather, be more adventurous and explore the potential for fun and friendship on the other side of your comfort zone.

Are you held back by doubts, fears, anxieties, or insecurities? You'll find it easier to say 'yes' to life and friends when you clear these blocks or emotional triggers. I used transformational tools including EFT (tapping), hypnotherapy, and NLP (neurolinguistic programming) to overcome my fear of the sea and heights so that I could be adventurous. If you're not equipped with the skills to do this yourself, check out Chapters 10 and 17 or seek help from an experienced therapist.

6. Say 'NO' more often

I also invite you to get more confident about speaking your truth and saying 'no' more, so you have time and energy to do things that will help you make good friends.

Do you ever say 'yes' only because you feel you 'should' or because you don't want to let people down? It's important to get your needs met in any relationship, and this involves saying 'no' when you want to.

Particularly if you're being put down, used, abused, or could be in danger. Others' expectations are just that. Their stuff, not yours. It's for you to decide what you want to do and to learn to say 'no' assertively to things you don't want to do. Find out how to say 'no' in Chapter 20.

7. Ask people out

Someone has to initiate all friendships. This could be inviting people out for a drink, or to do something together. The more you initiate friendships, the more friends you'll have (assuming you make smart friendship choices and are kind to your friends).

8. Move on to the next person when people don't reciprocate

A healthy friendship is a mutually joyful two-way relationship that needs to evolve at the right time for you both.

As you navigate the complexities of forging connections, remember that everyone's circumstances vary, influencing their ability to engage in new friendships. Time constraints, health issues, family commitments, or possessive partners, are examples of why they may not have the capacity for more friends. Yes, some people may feel you are not a good fit for each other, but that doesn't mean you're not perfect for others. We're all different. If someone says 'no' to meeting up or you get no response, move on to the next person. If it's a timing issue you can always try again in a few weeks or months.

9. Quality is more important than quantity of friendships

Fostering nourishing friendships with people who uplift you and bring out the best in you is more important than accumulating a multitude of superficial friends. Some people prefer a close-knit circle of five or six close friends. Others opt for an inner circle of intimate friends alongside lots of acquaintances or group contacts. The choice is yours.

10. Be curious, ask questions, and listen more than you talk

Adopt a curious approach to meeting people and learning new things. Instead of worrying about what to say, show genuine interest in others by asking questions and offering them the gift of active listening. Many people feel others don't listen to them enough and crave being heard.

Ask questions that invite people to tell you something interesting about themselves. You could ask them about things you want to do in the future to explore common interests. I share ideas for what to say and ask below.

Demonstrating genuine interest in others fosters richer interactions than speaking solely about yourself. As I used to say in communication skills courses, you have two ears and one mouth for a reason!

What to say when you first meet people

Your opening statements or questions influence the future scope and direction of the conversation.

Choose your story

In Chapter 11, I mentioned the importance of sharing a version of your story that reflects how you want others to perceive you and the future you want to live.

Ask questions

Match your initial questions to the setting, e.g. at a wedding you could ask 'Who do you know, the bride or groom?'

Not sure what to say? Come up with a list of questions in advance. You may find a box of conversation cards helpful. Or do an internet search to get the list of Art Arron's 36 Questions – designed to quickly create deep meaningful connections between two people.

Here are some ideas to get going:

- What brings you here?
- Who do you know here?
- How did you hear about this event?
- What do you like or think about...?
- Have you seen...?

If you know you're meeting certain people, find out something about them so you can ask more specific questions.

Avoid topics that are divisive and very personal questions – unless you're at an event where this is appropriate. Also be aware that asking people you've never met questions based on assumptions that don't apply to everyone can be triggering and bring up shame or upset for a lot of people, e.g. asking them if they have children or what they do for work.

Build your confidence with practice

Practise saying your story and questions out aloud to refine them so you feel more confident saying them to others.

What to say to invite people out

You only need a few ways to do this. As suggested above, come up with and practise in advance wording you can use so you feel more confident in the moment at asking people out. Ways to do this include:

- Do you fancy...?
- Would you like to...?
- Do you want to...?
- I'm thinking of... would you like to join me?

Key points

- There are many ways to meet and make new friends – in person or online. Focus on those that appeal the most to you.

- There's no point in only having ideas. The sooner you take action, the sooner you'll have more friends.

- If you're unsure what to say to people when you first meet them, prepare a list of questions in advance. You may even want to take them with you to remind yourself of them – not in front of people, but rather find a place to be alone and re-read them.

Activity: Write down ideas for where you could meet new like-minded people and simple questions you could ask them.

Chapter 15
Step 7 – Nurture Nourishing Friendships

Embrace uplifting habits so friendships flourish naturally

In this chapter, we delve into the art of nurturing relationships with friends, acquaintances, and new contacts. You can also apply what I share to family or business relationships.

Nurturing nourishing friendships involves developing highly effective habits and energising rituals – so your friendships flourish naturally and foster deep feelings of love, connection, and belonging. The aim is for these habits to become second nature and seamlessly fit into your life.

∾

I have one friend with whom I always arrange our next date when we're together. Early on in our friendship we realised this was the best way to ensure we see each other regularly. We put a date in the diary there and then and only change it in special circumstances. Should this happen, rather than cancelling, we postpone and put another date in our diaries straight away. She is now one of my closest and most cherished friends.

∾

Seven habits to nurture and maintain good friendships

1. Put friendship planning in your diary

Setting aside time to arrange to see or speak to friends can be pivotal in growing your friendship circle. This means making friends a priority, alongside all the other important things in your life, by setting aside time regularly in your diary – weekly, monthly, and/or annually. During this 'friendship planning' time, you consider which friends you want to see or connect with, and take action to reach out to them. It's also a good time to check birthdays, remember what's going on with friends who may need extra support, and consider other events with friends you need to prepare for. Do this at whatever frequency works best for you.

Most weeks, months, and years, I dedicate time to deciding who I want to see, visit, or call. While I connect with friends between these times, this is specifically when I sit down to be more proactive – calling or arranging meet-ups with people I've not seen for a while. Or reaching out to offer support. If I think of someone outside these periods, and it's not the right time to get in touch with them, I make a note in my diary to remind me the next time I'm doing friendship planning.

2. Turn your friendship planning into joyful rituals

To make your friendship planning a pleasurable experience, do this in uplifting environments. For instance, I love to sit on the beach or outside in my garden. Other times I put on our wood-burning stove and burn incense or a candle. I find doing this makes activities such as writing cards, letters, and emails more enjoyable.

It's also good to put yourself into a positive mental and emotional state before reaching out, so your words carry the energy of love, peace, and joy. You could meditate, go outside into nature, or do whatever you do to let go of stress or anxiety. Alternatively, reflect on why you're grateful for their friendship, or remember a fond memory you shared with them.

3. Be proactive in demonstrating you care

In Chapter 7, I shared how you can use the five love languages to demonstrate that you care: words, gifts, time, touch, and being of service.

You may be someone who learned how to do this when you were young, in which case it's likely to be something you don't need to consciously think about. However, I would suggest you consider how to express you care in all love languages, as we primarily do this in our style of preference which might be different to how your friends seek evidence you care.

$\sim$

A couple of years ago, a special friend sent me something that warmed my heart – photos of postcards I'd sent to her from around the world over thirty years ago. It was a lovely trip down memory lane. We met when I was seventeen and despite no longer living in the same country, and having led very different lives, we've kept in touch with postcards, letters, and visiting each other most years. What touched me most was not that my friend had kept these, but that she'd also let me know she'd found them while having a clear-out. Random surprise acts of kindness are a lovely way to nurture friendships.

$\sim$

4. Arrange your next call or meet-up every time you're with friends

You may not need to do this with people you see regularly or if you're part of a group that meets up regularly. However, it's definitely worth doing with friends you have to make more of an effort to see, perhaps because they live far away or because you both live busy lives. This habit could be the one thing that results in you enjoying a wonderful friendship rather than seeing that friendship ebbing away.

Where I don't do this with friends, it's usually because there's a rhythm to how we catch up.

5. Create regular rituals or experiences with friends

It's really nice to have regular activities or rituals you do with friends. This could be as simple as sending each other a 'checking in' text message each morning, going for a walk together at the same time each day or week, calling each other once a month, or enjoying a weekend away once a year.

When you do something for the first time, it's not a ritual... but it could become one. They often evolve naturally. Think about things you'd like to do and who you'd love to do them with. Then invite others to join you and see how you get on. If it works out well the first time, decide if you want to do it again. Ask yourself: what rituals with friends could I start?

6. Participate in group activities

Participating in group activities regularly, with like-minded people, is a good way to build friendships – especially if you have limited time. You could then also arrange to meet up with those you click with, on a one-to-one basis, so you can get to know them better. If you get on well, you may both decide you'd like to build a personal friendship, as well as being part of the group.

You could also create opportunities for groups of friends to come together regularly. It may be that you've met a group of people all at the same time, so coming together regularly as a group of friends makes sense. You could also bring together groups of people who don't know each other – people you think will get on and would appreciate meeting one another. I've set up a WhatsApp group of people who live locally so that when I fancy doing something, I can easily find out if others would like to join me.

7. Streamline and simplify

It's always good to find ways to make things easier and be more efficient with your time. Here are some ideas for streamlining and simplifying the process of nourishing friendships and showing people you care:

- **Use your diary** – to take a note of who you'll contact each month, birthdays, and special celebrations, so you're less likely to forget important dates and more likely to stay in touch with those important to you.

- **Bulk-buy a variety of cards** – for birthdays, anniversaries, and other occasions so you can respond quickly to important events and things that happen for your friends.

- **Bulk-buy special gifts** – when you find a gift you think several of your family and friends would like, buy enough to get you through the year.

- **Write personal newsletters** – people either love or hate these. Personally, I love receiving these from friends, as they keep me up-to-date with their lives. I used to write a short newsletter to put in my Christmas cards until a couple of years ago, when my dad died at Christmas and it felt like too much pressure. I'm not sure yet what I'll do going forward. Do what feels right.

Seven tips for nurturing nourishing friendships

As with meeting new people, there are a few things to remember which will influence the quality of friendships you have.

1. Prioritise people who make you feel good AND engage with you

Prioritising the right relationships is key. Once you know the type of friends you're looking for, you'll find it easier to nurture friendships with the right people – those who add joy to your life and help get your needs met. These are the people on the right-hand side of the friendship matrix we covered in Chapter 13.

As well as considering whether someone could be the type of friend you want, also be mindful of how interested others seem in you. Their level of interest in you early on can give insights into the type of friend they could be. This includes how they engage with you during conversations and how they respond to invitations to meet up.

- Are they listening to you, receptive to what you're saying, and actively participating in your conversation?
- Are they giving you their full attention?
- Is the conversation balanced with both contributing equally?

- Or does the other person consistently steer the conversation back to themselves?

2. Accept good friendships take time to flourish

Building worthwhile, meaningful friendships takes time. Rushing the process or expecting too much too soon can convey neediness, potentially causing others to withdraw. Instead, take the lead from the other person's behaviour and responses. Take one small step at a time.

Even with those you feel an instant connection, it can take time to get to know one another well. While some people may appreciate regular contact, others may retreat if they perceive the friendship is progressing too rapidly through frequent calls, texts, or requests. Occasionally, a wonderful friendship will evolve quickly. When it happens, treat this special bond as a bonus and celebrate it together.

3. Choose the best frequency and form for each friendship

How you define close friends is up to you, as is the best way to grow or maintain each friendship. Every friendship is unique. Discuss what works best for you and each friend.

4. Initiate more meet-ups

Through my observations and research, I've noted that individuals with fewer friends often aren't as proactive in initiating social interactions. This implies that once you've made connections with like-minded people, there's likely to be a pool of potential friends eagerly awaiting your invitation. If you don't ask people out, you could miss out on good friendships.

If you're naturally inclined to initiate social gatherings, it's important not to judge those who do not share this trait. Assuming mutual enjoyment of each other's company, it would be a shame to let such a small difference hinder potential friendships. Embracing the diversity of qualities and attributes we all possess is fundamental to cultivating meaningful connections, provided they do not pose harm to you or others.

5. End friendships that are not good for you

While meeting new people, you're likely to encounter people who are not right for you. Remember, making meaningful friendships is like dating – it's a process of getting to know people so you can assess your compatibility. You will get on with some people better than others and it's unrealistic to expect that everyone will become a friend.

If you find yourself in a relationship that isn't doing anything for you, trust your instincts and end it. Either let the other person know why you no longer want to be friends, or let the connection fade away naturally, as many friendships do. This will mean you'll have more time for nurturing relationships with people you want in your life. See Chapter 22.

6. Join events your contacts are going to

Sign up for activities and events that people you want to become friends with are going to. Sometimes, this may involve signing up for things you wouldn't usually go to or asking others what they're doing. Not stalking people, but rather just engaging more with people you know.

7. Nurture several relationships at the same time

Building several relationships at the same time can help ensure you get your needs met and can reduce the likelihood of you appearing needy.

Key points

- If you don't nurture relationships, you're missing out on friendships.

- Nurturing friends takes time but it's easier when you incorporate friendship habits into your everyday life.

- Put specific times in your diary or calendar for friendship planning so you remember to touch base with people you like and are important to you.

Activity: Note changes you could make to become better at nurturing nourishing friendships.

Part Three
Skills To Transform Your Friendships

Nourishing Friendships Workbook
Many of the following chapters have supporting practical exercises in my
Nourishing Friendships Workbook. This is available as a paperback on
Amazon or through my website: alisoun.com/friends

Chapter 16
Core Friendship Skills

Your skills transform the quality of your friendships

I hadn't planned to write this part of my book until the majority of people who completed my research survey said they wanted to know more about how to avoid, and better cope with, friendship challenges. And so the next series of chapters was born. Whether or not you've had any friendship challenges, the skills I share here apply to all relationships and aspects of life. I also hope you find the chapter of collective wisdom from women over sixty insightful.

We all have different personality traits, strengths and weaknesses that impact the quality of our relationships. In this chapter, I share a list of core skills that often enrich friendships. You don't need to master them all, but the more you embrace, the easier and more enjoyable your friendships and relationships are likely to be.

I was very fortunate to study interpersonal skills at university and then work for a company that trained me extensively on 'people' skills. Since setting up in business in 2003 as a well-being specialist, trainer, and coach, I've also invested heavily in personal development over the years. All this has been invaluable in enabling me to cope better with life's challenges and has influenced my choice of friends. That doesn't mean I'm perfect. Far from it. Like everyone else I'm human and sometimes make mistakes and unintentionally upset people. But I know I've got better at recognising the part I play, apologising, and being a better friend. I'm also more confident at standing up for myself when people are not treating me well – albeit though sometimes not soon enough, because I tend to see the best in others, I'm overly trusting, and want to help. I've learned, however, that the sooner I tackle issues, the easier it is to resolve them and move on.

Everyone does the best they can

Having an awareness of your skills and personality traits can give you greater insight into how you make a positive contribution to someone's life as a friend, as well as highlight areas for growth. It can also help you be more mindful and tolerant of others.

Everyone has different likes and preferences. Some people value courage, confidence, and directness, while others find the same qualities intimidating, cold, or challenging. That's why it's good to focus on building friendships with people who celebrate all aspects of the authentic person you are – the good and the bad.

At the heart of friendships is compassion. I believe we always do the best we can with the skills and resources available to us at any given time. When you believe this to be true, forgiveness, healing, and acceptance – of ourselves and others – is easier. Yes, there may be times you look back with hindsight and realise it would have been better to do something differently. But beating yourself up or feeling guilty doesn't help. Rather, learn how to accept that everyone does the best they can, and let go of any guilt or regret (see the next chapter).

You are never too old to make new friends

Some people believe it's too late to make new friends, change, or learn new skills, but that is simply a mindset. It is never too late to make new friends and embrace a new adventure – unless you're past your physical prime with aspirations of competing in the Olympics. In the context of friendship and the skills I share here, you're never too old and it's never too late!

Skills that make friendships easier

These skills will make friendships easier wherever you are on your friendship journey:

- **Self-esteem and confidence** – believing in yourself and your self-worth, and outwardly expressing this with confidence through your actions and behaviours.

- **Assertiveness** – standing up for yourself while respecting others, setting and affirming boundaries (see Chapter 19), and saying 'no' (see Chapter 20).

- **Positive mindset** – seeing the positive in situations, seeing the best in people, and being open to new opportunities and possibilities. This also involves reframing negative beliefs into positive statements, being open-minded, considering things from different perspectives, and focusing on what you can control and influence. We touched on this in Chapter 10.

- **Emotional resilience** – your ability to recognise and manage your emotions naturally so you can cope with life's challenges. Find out more in Chapter 17.

- **Personal leadership and responsibility** – taking personal responsibility for the part you play in situations, and seeking solutions rather than doing nothing, blaming others, or playing the victim. I explained this further in Chapter 7.

- **Heart-centered leadership** – acting from a place of love, kindness, and compassion, and striving to be the best, authentic version of yourself. This includes skills mentioned here plus trusting your intuition, optimising your energy, being of service, and embracing values such as honesty, authenticity, integrity, and trustworthiness. Check out my book on this topic: *Heartatude, the 9 Principles of Heart-Centered Success.*

- **Communication skills** – listening to what's said or not said, questioning, giving feedback, influencing, negotiating, and conflict resolution. How you communicate makes or breaks relationships. I cover some of these in following chapters.

- **Social skills** – being good at reading people, connecting with them, and adapting your communication style or focus to the person or situation. As well as confidently expressing kindness, empathy, compassion, and humility.

- **Relationship management** – your ability to be a good friend, make friends, nurture relationships, be supportive, show you care, end and rekindle friendships. Other important relationship skills include being able to bring out the best in others, give and take, compromise, share, and take turns.

As these are huge topics in themselves, I only touch on them in this book. My intention is to highlight skills that could enhance your friendships. You can learn more through reading books or attending workshops or courses. Many people also find the support of a coach or therapist helpful – especially if you want to make a significant change in your life, are entering a new stage of life, have mental health challenges or unresolved traumas, or your brain is wired in a particular way.

Play to your strengths

Focus on playing to your strengths in all your friendships, while also being mindful of your weaknesses. If you're unsure what either of these are, complete a simple skills assessment:

- **Start by creating a list of skills** – things you're good at, not good at, your personality traits, knowledge, ideal friendship qualities (from Chapter 12), and what you can contribute to friendships. Also add all the skills mentioned above to this list.

- **Rate yourself against each skill** – for each skill or trait listed, rate yourself on a scale of 0 to 10, with 0 being 'I'm a beginner' and 10 being 'I'm an expert'.

- **Celebrate your strengths** – consider how you can focus on what you're good at and make the most of these in friendships, e.g. in the way you make friends, or show friends that you care about them.

- **Decide which skills to learn or refine** – highlight which skills you feel could improve your friendships. These may be skills you've never learned, or skills to improve. Some skills are easier to learn than others, but if you ever face relationship challenges the effort will be worth it. You may also want to add new skills you'd love to learn that are nothing to do with friendships but where you might meet new people.

- **Commit to an action plan** – there's nothing like the present to create positive change in your life. Create and commit to a plan for reading books or attending classes/courses.

Key Points

- Your skills or lack of them influence ALL your relationships and your friendships.

- The more skills you master, the easier you'll find your friendships.

- It's never too late to learn skills or create new habits that will improve your friendships and life.

Activity: Consider what skills it could be worth refining – you never know, you might make friends along the way!

Chapter 17
Manage Your Emotions

Being able to change how you feel naturally is a life-changer

Your ability to manage your emotions naturally improves all areas of your life, including the quality of your friendships. Think about it. Have you ever been:

- Stressed and taken it out on a friend?
- Upset or triggered by what a friend said or did?
- Surprised by the way a friend has reacted?

We've all had unique life experiences, so we naturally all bring different perspectives, behaviours, and emotional triggers into our friendships. These can sometimes unintentionally lead to upsets, frustration, misunderstandings, and for some friendships to end unnecessarily.

In this chapter, I share healthy ways to let go of negative emotions so you can feel better and take fewer emotional issues into relationships with you.

If you already adopt unhealthy strategies to make you feel better, such as drinking alcohol, taking drugs, comfort eating, having a treat, or buying something new, you can also learn how to change how you feel naturally and develop healthy habits. Not only will this influence the type of friends you attract, but your relationships are likely to be easier and more fulfilling too.

You can learn to manage your emotions naturally

I remember the first time someone told me that I could transform my life by managing my thoughts and feelings. I didn't believe them. I thought they were being glib and had no idea about what I was going through.

Then the penny dropped. I realised I was already doing things to make myself feel better: spending time buying things I didn't need, comfort eating, and drinking too much alcohol. I knew they weren't the best long-term strategies but hadn't realised there was an alternative.

Once I learned to be kinder to myself, believe in myself, and manage my emotions better, I started making smarter choices, aligned with what I wanted and what was good for me. For the first time ever, I felt happier and more in control of my life.

Since that day in 2001, I have taught thousands of people how to manage their emotions naturally and create the life they want for themselves. I've worked with people of all ages and varied life experiences, including people with depression, bipolar disorder, and genocide survivors.

Most recently, I've been helping midlife women overcome stress, burnout, and loneliness, a lack of purpose, and the upset of being childless – so they can enjoy a happy, meaningful life that they will look back on with pride. Many now feel better about themselves, their friendships, and their lives. Having witnessed their transformations, I'm in awe of our human capacity to heal and recreate ourselves. It's just that most people aren't taught how to do this intentionally.

Experiencing a range of emotions is healthy

It's human to experience a range of feelings, from grief, shock, and anger, to peace, love, joy, and confidence. Managing your emotions effectively isn't about always trying to be positive or to deny how you feel; it's about being mindful of how you feel and allowing yourself to experience all emotions appropriately. It also involves recognising when it would be healthy to proactively change how you feel – so you can feel better, live better, and respond better. This includes letting go of negative emotions that don't serve you, and activating positive emotions you'd like to feel, such as confidence, assertiveness, or optimism.

Change how you feel in the moment

How you feel emotionally is a complex topic that includes all sorts of things, including your hormonal balance, what you eat, drink, and your body's ability to process what you eat and drink, how and when you exercise, your sleep patterns, who you spend time with, and the environments you choose to be in, e.g. relationships, and where you work. Some aspects of these you can control and influence, but others you cannot, such as how your brain is wired, your genetic make-up, and certain life events.

The focus in this chapter is to consider what you can do to change how you feel in the moment; a bit like taking a tablet to get rid of a headache.

Most people have experienced upset or trauma to some extent that result in intense negative emotions (triggers) which can sabotage relationships – unless they are released and healed. If you regularly experience conflict in relationships, that's feedback that you could have emotional triggers to clear. There are many ways to let go of emotional triggers from the past, so that they're not activated again in the future. The only technique I share in this book that has this potential is Emotional Freedom Technique (EFT or tapping).

Refreshing emotional truths

- It's not what happens to you that determines how you feel, but how you choose to respond to people or situations, albeit often at a subconscious level.

- Other than in the acute stages of shock, trauma, or grief, you can change how you feel naturally, so you can feel better and cope better.

- You can always take steps to let go of negative feelings you feel in response to others or situations, like upset, hurt, guilt, jealousy, or disappointment.

- There are many ways to change how you feel naturally, some of which you may already do. Perhaps you enjoy sport or some kind of exercise, play uplifting or calming music, go for a walk, or engage in other 'feel-good' activities. Or visit a park, forest, or beach. The trick is to consciously adopt healthy, feel-good strategies to put yourself in a positive emotional state ahead of engaging with others – unless you're in the early stages of grief, trauma, or shock (when it's healthy to feel that way) or are turning to people for support.

Five simple ways to feel good naturally

These techniques help you to release negative emotions and feel better, in most situations.

To make it easier for you to use these techniques, I've also recorded a free series of five videos, each demonstrating a different method. You can check them out at alisoun.com/friends

1. Move

Every emotion is linked to a specific posture and a unique blend of hormones. The simplest way to change how you feel, in a way your body understands, is to adjust your physiology (how you're standing or sitting) to match how you want to feel, e.g. to let go of nerves and feel more confident. When you adopt the posture or stance associated with that emotion, your body sends a message to your brain to release the hormonal cocktail that creates that feeling. You can move or change your posture to shift your emotional state at any time for any emotion.

Practical exercise: your confident posture

Take a moment to imagine you're feeling nervous or anxious, and adopt the physical posture you associate with these feelings, whether standing or sitting. Hold this posture for a few seconds and notice how you feel. Next, imagine feeling confident. Adjust your physiology to reflect confidence –

stand tall, hold your head high, and smile. Notice the shift in your feelings. Do you feel more confident or self-assured? As you maintain this confident stance, notice how it's more difficult to feel nervous.

An extension of this is to smile. It may sound simple, but smiling – even when you don't feel good – can alter your emotional state. When you smile, the muscles in your face signal to your brain to release hormones associated with happiness. Try it now: imagine feeling happy, sit or stand tall, and physically smile. Now, attempt to feel nervous or anxious while holding this smiling posture. It's surprisingly difficult. Smiling before responding to people or situations can enhance your mood and improve your interactions with them.

2. Breathe

When you're feeling anxious or nervous, you likely find yourself breathing quickly from your upper chest. A simple yet powerful way to calm yourself is through breath work. There are various methods for doing this, some of which you may already know if you attend yoga, meditation, or relaxation classes.

Practical exercise: even breathing

Whether standing up or lying down, place one hand on your chest and the other on your stomach. Begin by focusing on your breath. Notice the pace – fast or slow? After a few moments, start to breathe in and out to a count of 3: inhale for 3 counts, exhale for 3 counts. Gradually slow down your breathing. Work towards inhaling for 5 counts and exhaling for 5 counts and keep doing this for a few minutes. Notice how you feel throughout and after doing this.

3. Use your imagination

Your imagination is one of the most powerful tools you have, because your brain cannot distinguish between what you actually do physically and what you imagine doing. In both cases, you create physical neural-pathways in your brain.

This is why visualisation is hugely popular among top athletes worldwide. Across all sports, athletes imagine performing perfectly in their heads, as part of their training regime and immediately before competing.

If you imagine things going wrong, you're more likely to experience setbacks. Conversely, visualising things going the way you want increases the likelihood of success. While you may not have control over outcomes, harnessing the power of your imagination can improve your confidence beforehand and increase your chances of achieving your desired results.

Practical exercise: mental rehearsal

Ahead of participating in activities you find challenging, visualise the entire experience going exceptionally well in your mind. Picture yourself feeling confident, enjoying meaningful conversations, and adeptly handling any challenges that may arise. Repeat this visualisation exercise several times, leading up to the event.

4. Change your thoughts with active affirmations

In Chapter 10, I discussed how your thoughts directly influence your emotions and outlined strategies for cultivating a positive mindset, such as focusing on what you can control and influence, and practising affirmations.

Practical exercise: simple affirmations:

- It's possible to make lots of lovely new friends.
- I can have fun trying out new things and making friends.
- I deserve to be surrounded by friends who will love me as much as I do them.

To boost the power of your affirmations, make them personal and specific, and recite them aloud while engaging in empowering physical actions. I guide you through a practical exercise to create personal affirmations in the Nourishing Friendships Workbook that accompanies this book.

5. Emotional Freedom Technique (EFT or tapping)

Tapping is a remarkably quick and effective tool to change how you feel in the moment and let go of emotional trauma and triggers from the past, so that you naturally feel better and cope better in the future. It has gained popularity in aiding individuals who have undergone severe trauma, such as war veterans, survivors of terrorist attacks, natural disasters, and war, and emergency responders. Thankfully, it's also becoming increasingly available to everyone.

Often described as acupuncture without needles, tapping involves using your fingers to gently tap on specific points on your head and body. Doing this helps to release negative emotions, beliefs, memories, and physical pain. Tapping stands out as being the most powerful intervention, especially for deeper emotional release.

For a more comprehensive explanation of how tapping works, read my book, *Heartatude: The 9 Principles of Heart-Centered Success.* Or check out my demonstration video in the Feel Good Video series at alisoun.com/friends

Using these techniques

Whenever you feel nervous, anxious, stressed, hurt, or any other negative emotion, STOP and pause before engaging or responding. Don't respond when you're upset or angry. Taking a few moments to stop, reflect, and intentionally change how you feel, can make all the difference. Or sleep on it if need be.

Try the techniques I share above, or consider other ways to create a positive emotional state – such as listening to uplifting music, dancing or singing along to a song that uplifts you – before interacting with others or attending an event. We're all unique, so experiment with different strategies until you discover the ones that work best for you.

Help is available

Learning how to manage your emotions naturally is something everyone can do. However, it is also a complex topic, as there are many reasons you might not feel good, such as extreme trauma, challenging life experiences, and various health conditions.

Some people find it intuitive to manage their emotions naturally but many discover it's easier to learn how to do this through therapy or by attending personal development workshops or classes. It's only because I've spent years training and working as a therapist and coach, and teaching others, that this is now second nature to me... most of the time.

If you've experienced severe trauma or face complex health issues, and you want to boost your emotional or mental well-being, I suggest you explore available support through your healthcare provider. You can also search online for therapists, workshops, or support groups.

Key points

- Negative emotions and behaviours can strain friendships. If you want to enjoy better friendships, learn how to release any self-sabotaging emotions.

- It's possible to change how you feel naturally – in most situations.

- Equipping yourself with a toolkit of preferred techniques can profoundly enhance both your life and your friendships.

Activity: Practise changing how you feel, and decide whether it would be beneficial to work with a therapist to boost your emotional well-being and friendships.

Free Feel Good Video Series
To make it easier for you to practise these techniques, I've recorded a series of short videos. Check this out at alisoun.com/friends

Chapter 18
Communication Skills

The world would be a better place if everyone was a confident, compassionate communicator

Have you ever been worried about what to say? Or found someone misunderstood what you said?

Communication is one of the most underrated skills, and yet so valuable for us all to learn.

〜

I used to think I was a good communicator until I attended communication, influencing, and negotiation skills training courses through work. Now also as a trained hypnotherapist, NLP Master Practitioner, and experienced public speaker, I realise that the communication skills I learned when growing up, only took me to a basic functional level of competency. I now know my natural communication style, strengths and weaknesses, how to spot the same in others, and can better adapt my communications for different people and situations. Being human, I sometimes still get it wrong, but when I do I consider the part I played so I can learn from the experience.

〜

In this chapter, I touch on a few core communication principles and skills which it's helpful to master so you find it easier to enjoy good friendships. This builds upon knowing what to say when you first meet people or want to invite people out (see Chapter 14). You'll also find suggested wording for saying 'no' in Chapter 20, and ending friendships in Chapter 22.

We naturally misinterpret most communications

At my communication skills courses I used to do a simple exercise that highlights how easy it is to misinterpret communications. It only involves six of the most basic words in the English language, yet it always managed to stun audiences. I would ask attendees to close their eyes and think about the statement: 'the cat sits on the mat'. After thirty seconds, I'd ask them to open their eyes and tell me what they'd seen, heard, or felt. Some people saw images. Others didn't. There were also various types and colours of cats. Some cats were on a mat, others were in front of a fire, or on a doorstep. People who thought about one of their cats often felt good. Others found themselves thinking, *I don't like cats,* or feeling anxious.

You see, there is no right and wrong – we all interpret the same message differently because we all have different life experiences. This means there's always a gap between an intended message and how another person interprets it – even with the most basic statements.

Imagine the scope for misinterpretations when you take into account:

- More complex ideas.
- Diverse life experiences.
- Trauma, emotional triggers, or trust issues.
- A lack of self-esteem or confidence.
- Physical and mental health issues.
- Cultural differences.
- Different communication styles, e.g. detail versus big picture, introvert versus extrovert, or people-focused versus task-focused.
- Privilege and the lack of awareness for people who will never have what you take for granted.

The more complex or longer the communication, the more scope there is for people to misinterpret your intended message and to react adversely. So, it's remarkable that we seem to communicate with each other relatively well most of the time.

Skilled communicators know how to close the gap between intended and interpreted messages with even the most complex of communications. They are also good at picking up what's not being said, getting to the truth of a situation, and adapting their style to that of the person or people they want to reach. Advanced communication skills include conflict resolution, negotiation, presentation, hypnosis, and compassionate and trauma-informed communication.

Communication is far more than your words

In face-to-face communications, only 7% of how someone interprets what you say comes from your words; 38% of their understanding comes from your tonality (the way you say things); and 55% comes from your body language.

You always communicate the truth of a situation unconsciously through your tonality and body language – unless you are consciously managing these non-verbal cues. If there is a misalignment between your body language, tonality, and your words, people don't believe the words you are saying.

For example, if you asked someone how they were and they barked 'fine' while shaking their head and scowling, you could tell from their body language they weren't fine. Likewise, we may doubt or not have confidence in people who appear nervous or doubtful, yet believe exactly the same words being said by a person who projects more authority (e.g. smiling, standing tall, or speaking in a firm, nicely audible, and confident tone).

Any misalignment between your words, tonality, and body language also leads people to question your honesty, integrity, and trustworthiness.

The energy behind your words gives them meaning

It's the energy behind what you say that gives your words meaning. In other words, when you have a positive intention, such as wanting the best for the other person, you're likely to communicate with tonality and body language that also express this. However, if you are critical, jealous, or judgemental, this is what people will hear in your response – even if you say the right words. That's not to say your choice of words isn't important. Of course it is. But it's critical to also be aware of your tonality and body language, and the impact these have on how others respond to you.

That's why managing your emotions and putting yourself in a calm and kind emotional state *before* responding or interacting with others can be so important. Especially if you often unintentionally get into arguments or upset people – because your feelings drive your actions and behaviours.

I shared ways to manage your emotions in the last chapter. Another simple tool is to ask yourself the following question before communicating anything, 'What is my positive intention in saying or doing this?' If your answer aligns with the message you want to get across, that's good. Sometimes, however, asking ourselves this question can highlight our original desired outcome didn't come from a place of love or kindness, and that there is something better we could say or do.

Consistent communications

Communicating with friends isn't just about isolated conversations. The quality of relationships also often depends upon the consistency of your communications. This includes:

- How you communicate with one another.
- The frequency and format of communications that works best for you both.
- How you show up in conversations, e.g. are you usually supportive, loving, and kind, or defensive, critical, or argumentative?

When you are consistently kind, loving, and compassionate, people are more likely to tolerate if you have an off day, act out of character, or forget something important.

Ten communication tips to boost your friendships

Here are ten ways to boost your communication skills and friendships.

1. Define your desired outcomes and positive intentions

Ahead of every important communication consider what you want for yourself and others. Refrain from saying things where you realise your desired outcomes or intentions are not positive, e.g. if you want to prove the other person is wrong when it's about something unimportant.

2. Put yourself in a positive emotional state

Connect to your heart and put yourself in an emotional state of peace, love, kindness, and compassion before engaging with others. This is particularly important if you feel negative emotions, such as anger, frustration, hurt, or upset. Letting go of these negative emotions can help you avoid saying the wrong things you'll later regret.

3. Facilitate two-way conversations

Conversations are a dance of words, tonality, and body language between two or more people. Speaking *at* people can come across as being self-centred and drive them away. Asking people questions without sharing anything about yourself can come across as intense. So, it's best to balance a mix of talking, asking questions, and listening.

4. Repeat your understanding communications

To close the gap between others' intended messages versus how you interpret them, you can repeat back your understanding of what they've just said. For example, you could say, 'So am I right in thinking (repeat back what they've said)?' Use exactly the same words the other person has said to minimise any friction. This gives the other person the opportunity to let you know if they meant something different.

5. Speak your truth with compassion

This includes saying all you want to say, and saying 'no' when appropriate (see Chapter 20). When you disagree with something, e.g. what someone's said or done, or not said or done, it's healthy to speak up. Failing to speak your truth often causes bigger problems in the future.

6. Practise active listening

Being a good active listener involves being fully present in the moment so that you can hear what's being said and not said. Cues which demonstrate you're listening include natural eye contact, accurately repeating back what your friend has said, and asking questions that show you're listening. Observe and listen to the other person's responses and address any misunderstandings as they happen. Active listening also means putting away all potential distractions such as your mobile phone, computer, or books, allowing you to truly listen and show genuine interest.

7. Ask the right questions

Match the type of question you use to your desired outcomes. Use open questions when you want people to share more about themselves or a situation. These usually begin with how, what, or why. Or use closed questions when there is a definitive answer such as yes, no, or their name. Avoid asking questions that show you haven't been listening.

8. Manage your words, tonality, and body language

Most people focus on thinking about what they want to say to people without giving much conscious thought about their body language or tonality. Yet words only account for 7% of the way in which others interpret face-to-face communications. So, ahead of conversations also consider how to use your body language and tone to communicate a message consistent to the words you intend to say.

9. Consider things from the other person's perspective

We all have different motivations, skill sets, needs, values, desires, and communication styles. When you communicate your message in a way that's aligned to the other person's perspective, and how they could be feeling, they are more likely to respond positively.

10. Take responsibility for your part in all communications

When you're in a relationship with others, you always have a part to play when things between you both go well but also when there are differences of opinions and upsets. Be prepared to say sorry for any unintentional upset or misunderstanding you may cause.

If you're someone who communicates in ways others often consider blunt or insensitive, because of how your brain is wired, you could let your friends know this in advance. Some may really value your direct honesty.

Also recognise that if you're really upset about something someone has done or not done, you may have an emotional trigger from the past which you've yet to heal.

Key points:

- We naturally miscommunicate with each other all the time, therefore double check critical details by repeating back your understanding of what's just been said.

- The better your communication skills, the less friction you're likely to experience in your friendships. A few simple tweaks can make all the difference.

- The meaning of your communications is the results you get. If you're not getting the results you want, consider the part you have played in this and what you could do differently.

Activity: Consider your strengths and weaknesses when it comes to communicating with others, and decide whether it would be beneficial to refine these.

Chapter 19
Setting Boundaries With Friends

What you think about me is none of my business

Are you a people-pleaser who struggles to say 'no' to friends?

Do you ever feel friends treat you in ways you don't like?

Or do you feel overwhelmed as you've over-committed yourself?

Friendships are easier when you set and communicate clear boundaries. Doing this often helps avoid unnecessary stress, upsets, and friendships turning toxic or breaking down completely.

∽

I remember needing to speak to someone about the way they were treating me. This person was a bully – not just towards me, but to others in a group. I was dreading the conversation but somehow found the courage to tell them what behaviours I wasn't willing to accept, and what I needed from them. What surprised me the most was that the person started treating me better, yet continued in the same vein with others who didn't stand up to them. That was a huge eye-opener to me on the power of setting boundaries.

∽

What is a boundary?

Relationship boundaries are what you need to feel safe and happy in a relationship. They are reflected in the choices and decisions you make every day, your actions, behaviours, and how you stand up for yourself when others are not respecting your needs. Unlike physical boundaries, relationship boundaries are not obvious to others, because we all have different needs, values, and preferences. That's why it's always helpful to communicate your boundaries to others.

The boundary spectrum

At one end of the spectrum, you have people with firm boundaries that stop others from getting close. The downside of rigid boundaries is that you push people away – if they don't feel they can connect with you emotionally.

At the other end of the spectrum are people-pleasers who put others' needs and desires before themselves with no self-love, self-respect, or boundaries. Unfortunately, if you don't ensure your own needs are met, you're more likely to feel overwhelmed, burnt out, disappointed, hurt, upset, resentful, frustrated, jealous, or angry. You're also easy prey for people wanting to manipulate and control you. Both ends of the spectrum come from a place of fear, lack, or insecurity.

In the middle of the spectrum are healthy boundaries based on love, kindness, compassion, honesty, integrity, and respect – towards yourself and others. When you choose to have healthy boundaries you:

- Have your needs met through how you engage with others.
- Honour your needs and don't give in to peer pressure.
- Communicate your boundaries to others.
- Stand up for yourself assertively, as needed.
- Take responsibility rather than blaming others.
- Honour others' boundaries – as much as you can without compromising your own needs.
- Listen to others' perspectives rather than being obsessed with showing that you're right and they are wrong.

Boundaries versus expectations

Some people refer to their expectations of how they hope to be treated by others as their boundaries, placing the responsibility on the other person. But boundaries are for YOU to decide, communicate, and apply to ensure that your needs are met. The onus is on you, not the other person. Yes, you may want others to respect your needs, but how can they do this if you don't communicate your needs to them?

Expectations are weaker than boundaries. Having expectations of others often leads to feelings of frustration, hurt, anger, or disappointment. They often also carry the energy of judgement, while boundaries carry a positive energy of you stepping into your personal power. By affirming clear boundaries, you increase the likelihood that you'll be treated in the way you want to be.

The scope of friendship boundaries

Needs and boundaries cover different areas of life, including:

- **Physical boundaries** – these relate to what you need and want physically, e.g. sleep (getting enough and being able to rest), nutrition (being able to eat what you want and need), personal space, and physical touch (or not). An example of a physical boundary being compromised is if you need to avoid alcohol, yet you have a glass of wine or allow others to pressurise you into having a drink. Likewise, if you want to stick to a specific diet, yet give in to your cravings or others egging you on to eat something else.

- **Emotional boundaries** – relate to how you want to feel. They include your need to feel safe expressing your views or how you're feeling, your ability to say 'no' to events you don't want to attend, to be your true self, or to stand up for yourself if someone violates one of your boundaries. Plus, knowing where and when to have emotionally charged conversations.

- **Time boundaries** – these include turning up on time, honouring agreed timeframes and limitations, and respecting when people are not available or need time for themselves or other commitments.

- **Intellectual/topical boundaries** – respecting differing opinions (agreeing to disagree) and cultures, being open-minded, not forcing your opinions on others or putting people down, not making others feel 'less than' or deliberately hurting others. Knowing when it's appropriate to talk about certain things, and what topics to stay away from.

- **Material boundaries** – relate to people using or borrowing your belongings and the limitations you want to place around these.

Other boundaries include sexual boundaries and financial boundaries.

How to set boundaries

Use this process to set robust boundaries with friends so that you and others can honour them.

- **Get clear on your needs** – at the core of your boundaries are your needs, values, and desired outcomes. Start by listing your core needs – for you personally. Example: I need 8 hours of sleep a night.

- **Define boundaries for each need** – what do you need to put in place in order to have that specific need met? Example: My boundary is to be in bed by 9.30pm every weeknight.

- **Apply your boundaries through your actions** – you can demonstrate your boundaries through your actions (personal standards). Example: I commit to going to bed by 9.30pm every weeknight. Then do it.

- **Communicate your boundaries to others verbally** – as and when needed. Example: if someone asks you out to a late-night concert you could say, 'I need to be in bed by 9.30pm during the week so thanks but I'll give that a miss.'

Setting and planning how to communicate healthy boundaries enables you to feel comfortable and confident when engaging with others. When others respect your boundaries, you feel good.

Define your healthy friendship boundaries

Come up with a list of critical and desirable boundaries based on your needs. To do this, consider:

- How you need and want to be treated.
- What makes a good friendship for you – as you explored in Chapters 7 and 12.
- Unacceptable behaviours (you may get some ideas for these from Chapter 7) which you can convert into boundaries.
- Behaviours that trigger you.
- What you need and want from a friendship.
- Restraints or limitations on what you can offer as a friend.
- Whether you like or dislike physical touch.
- Your greeting preference, e.g. a hug, smile, handshake, or kiss on the cheek.
- Your preferred form of communication, e.g. by phone, in person, or by message.

Be aware of fear-based boundaries which you feel you need to put in place to protect yourself from danger. These are obviously understandable where you've experienced trauma in the past, or your brain works a certain way. However, if you put up barriers to friendship that are too rigid, you may come across as being too distant, detached, or unavailable, and push potentially good friends away. Friendships need vulnerability, connection, and trust to flourish. And people need to feel they can get to know you and connect with you.

The aim is to have a core set of boundaries which apply to all relationships. You might, though, have additional boundaries you feel you need to put in place for specific situations or people. For example, if your best friend is also your boss, it's worthwhile clarifying boundaries for both your working and personal relationships.

Communicate your boundaries

Many of us share similar friendship boundaries, e.g. the need to be treated with love and kindness. But this lulls people into a false sense of security, meaning they don't communicate boundaries to friends.

However as we all have differing needs, others can't possibly know yours until you tell them; as a result misunderstandings and conflicts can often arise. That's why it can be helpful to discuss boundaries with friends – particularly the less obvious needs such as your preference with regard to physical touch, or your availability for friendship. Communicating your boundaries also helps to minimise challenging situations. And you do this through what you say and do – whether in the general course of conversation or in a more specific discussion.

If you want others to respect your boundaries, you need to act in alignment with these. Otherwise, you send mixed messages and increase the likelihood of someone mistreating or manipulating you. For example, if someone puts you down and you do nothing, you are effectively communicating to them that it's OK for them to treat you that way. Doing this over time feeds unhealthy relationships.

What to do when someone violates a boundary

As soon as you feel you're being mistreated, it's vital you address the situation to avoid it turning into a bigger issue – particularly if you feel someone has been disrespectful, used you, hurt you, or abused you. I share ideas for how to do this effectively in the next chapter.

Saying 'no' to boundary violations is a powerful way to say 'yes' to your self-care and the relationships you want to have. You deserve to be treated with love, kindness, and respect. And those who don't treat you this way, do not deserve to have you as a friend.

By clarifying what's acceptable to you (and not), you step into your personal power and become more assertive in the friendship dynamic.

Honour others' boundaries

Friendships are two-way relationships. You need people to treat you well and others need the same from you. The challenge can be if your boundaries differ and you haven't discussed this. If you're not sure what others' boundaries are, ask for clarification. Also, have the confidence to speak up and affirm your needs if someone wants you to do something that compromises them.

Key points

- Your boundaries reflect what you need and want from others. It's for you to take action to ensure these are met.

- As soon as someone mistreats you or violates one of your boundaries, speak to them to avoid the situation escalating.

- Honouring others' boundaries is important too, as long as this doesn't mean compromising your own critical needs.

Activity: List all your friendship needs and boundaries so that you're clear on these and can confidently communicate them to others.

Chapter 20
Say 'No' Without Feeling Guilty

If you don't prioritise your time, others will

I wonder if there's ever been a time when you wanted to say 'no' but found yourself saying 'yes'?

Maybe you felt that you 'should' do something for fear of upsetting or letting people down, or were worried about what others would think of you if you said 'no'– because you want people to think of you as a nice rather than a selfish person.

Additionally, for hundreds of years women across most cultures, and people from minority groups, have been conditioned to conform, to be quiet, do what they're told, and act in ways expected by a more dominant male society.

Most of us have been conditioned to believe that nice people are always there for others, and that by saying 'no' or setting boundaries you're selfish or not a good person. If you believe this to be true, you will be caught in the trap of saying 'yes' and compromising your own needs simply to get external validation from people.

The reality is, though, you can still be a good kind person and:

- Stand up for yourself.
- Set boundaries.
- Say 'no'.
- Challenge people who mistreat you or others.
- Walk away from unhealthy situations and friendships.
- Make mistakes and upset people unintentionally.
- Apologise.
- Love and respect yourself.
- Put yourself first when you need to.
- Do all of this without needing to explain why!

It's time we all stood up and said 'no' more often and collectively chip away at outdated misogynistic, racist, sexist, and ageist societal privileges and norms. When you say 'yes' and put others' needs and expectations before your own, you are effectively saying they are more important than you. And this comes at a cost to your happiness and well-being. Think back to a time when you said 'yes' but wanted to say 'no'. How did you feel?

The costs of saying 'yes' when you want to say 'no'

When you say 'yes' rather than 'no' you:

- Waste time you could spend with people important to you.

- Fritter away money you could put to better use or invest in things you'd like to do with friends.

- Drain your energy and limit your capacity.

- Make feelings of resentment, overwhelm, frustration, anger, and other negative emotions worse.

- Corrode your physical, mental, and emotional health .

Yet you could avoid these costs by saying 'no'. In this chapter, you'll discover how to say 'no' without feeling guilty – so you feel more empowered and in control of your life. This involves applying healthy boundaries and communicating with others using language that's most likely to be received well.

Create a better future: say 'no' appropriately

Imagine how things could be different if you felt confident saying 'no'.

- What are the benefits of saying 'no' – to you and those you care about?

- How would you feel if the other person accepted 'no'?

- How would you feel knowing you've done the right thing, irrespective of the other person's response?

You already know how to physically say 'no'

If you can physically say the word 'no', it means when you feel reluctant to do so that the only things holding you back are your doubts and emotions – fears about saying 'no', or being unsure how to say 'no' in a way that is most likely to be heard and accepted in the way you intend.

Be intentional about how you say 'no'

There are different ways to do this:

- Say 'no' with no further explanation. There is no need for you to justify your decision. 'No' is a complete sentence!

- Explain why and offer alternative solutions. You may find the following UHT model useful for this.

- Be direct and straight to the point when you think this is the best way to get your point across.

The UHT model

This is a simple yet powerful model which will help you say 'no' assertively, but with kindness and compassion. You can use this to:

- Say 'no' to doing something you can't/don't want to do.
- Discontinue a relationship or friendship.
- Reaffirm boundaries when people mistreat you.
- Change the direction of a conversation.
- Express a different point of view.
- Negotiate the best time to connect.
- Communicate why something/someone isn't for you.

Breaking down the UHT model

- U = I understand (repeat back your understanding)
- H = However (why you can't or aren't willing to do it)
- T = Therefore (offer a solution or alternative)

- **I understand** – repeating what you've heard can help avoid misunderstandings, upsets, and friction, especially in critical situations. It also helps the other person to feel heard and allows them to let you know if they meant something different. The easiest way to do this is to use exactly the same words people use when speaking to you. For instance, if they say they want to see you this weekend, you repeat back, 'I understand you want to see me this weekend'. Alternative words for 'understand' include: hear, see, realise, agree, or get. You could also say 'It's very kind of you,' or 'I agree it's been nice.' Or simply say 'thanks'.

- **However** – this is where you explain your reason for saying 'no'. An alternative to 'however' is 'but'.

- **Therefore** – if you feel it's appropriate or helpful, you can end with a solution or a way forward. Alternatives to saying 'therefore' include: so, perhaps, maybe, and let's.

~

Years ago I remember someone invited me to an event I didn't fancy. I'd heard she often hosted this type of event and was concerned that if I said 'yes' once, I'd keep being invited to future events. Likewise, I was concerned about saying 'no' without giving her a reason. I decided it was best to tell her the truth, using this model. I responded, 'Thanks for your invite, but that isn't my cup of tea. So, let's get together another time.' She was fine with this.

~

While it's important to use words and phrases that reflect who you are, let's first look at the basic structure before variations of this:

- Thanks for inviting me to the cinema tonight. I'd love to come but I've things I need to do. How about we put a time in our diaries now to go and see the film next week?

- I hear you'd like me to pop around later, but I'm not feeling well. I'll get in touch when I'm feeling better.

- I've enjoyed your company, and it would be great to see you again, but it sounds like our diaries clash at the moment.

- I'd love to get to know you better, but I've got a lot of things over the next few weeks. I'll be in touch when things change.

- I'd love to come out on Saturday but evenings are not good for me. Perhaps we could do lunchtime instead?

- It's been great chatting with you, but I'm looking for friends who live nearby. So, let's just stay connected via social media at the moment.

- I'm grateful for the part you've played in my life, but it's not OK for you to treat me like that. Don't contact me again.

- It's nice of you to ask, but I don't have the capacity at the moment. How about asking (name) instead?

- I hear you don't like (name), but I'm not interested in bitching about them. Let's talk about something else.

- I hear and respect your views on, e.g. the COVID-19 vaccine. However, I don't like being preached at or shouted at. If you want this friendship to continue, let's agree to disagree and talk about something else.

- I know you're keen to go away for a weekend with (name), but she's not my kind of person. Let's arrange to go away together another time, just the two of us.

- I hear you're having a difficult time but I'm not happy about how you treat me. So let's take a break and see how we feel in a couple of months.

- I know you don't know many people here but we seem to have very different views and approaches to life. I'm sure you'll find other people who you'll connect with much better.

Being direct and straight to the point

Being direct is sometimes a better way forward, especially with people who are direct themselves. You can do this using just one or two parts of the above model. These are more direct versions of the above responses:

- No.
- No thanks.
- No, I don't want to.
- No. This has been fun but once is enough.
- I can't come around this weekend but I'll come to see you next week.
- I'm sorry but I don't have time to invest in new friendships.
- Thanks for asking, but that's not for me.

- I'm not feeling well so I'll give it a miss.
- I'd love to meet up again, but it sounds like we're not available at the same times of the week.
- This friendship isn't working for me.
- Stop speaking to me like that.
- Stop putting me down.
- Do not contact me again.
- That sounds fun, but I have a lot going on at home/work.
- Now isn't a good time for me. I'll let you know if things change.
- I'm sorry, I'm already going with someone else.
- I feeling overwhelmed with all I've got on right now. I'll see you in class next week.
- I enjoyed seeing you, but I'm too busy to commit to more right now.
- I'm not interested, but I'm sure someone else would love to go.
- No, I'm sorry, I need to prioritise my family/work/business/health right now.
- I've been spending too much money lately. Can we do something else?
- Agreeing to do that would compromise my values, so no.
- I'm going to pass this time. Perhaps another time.

There's more to saying 'no' than your words

Remember, there is more to communication than words, as explained in Chapter 18. So, it's critical that your tone and your body language reflect the same message. If there are any inconsistencies, the other person will know you're nervous or that you don't mean what you're saying.

Letting go of 'shoulds' and others' expectations

When you feel you need to meet others' expectations, it's common to feel you 'should' do something rather than honouring your own desires and saying 'no'. These 'should' feelings usually come from years of programming from a young age, by parents, carers, culture, or religion. When we are young, we conform to others' expectations, as we often depend on the people imposing them. As an adult, though, you have choices you didn't have as a child. And you may find that some of these 'shoulds' are based on outdated unconscious beliefs or emotional triggers which no longer serve you.

It's time to step into your own power and either choose to say 'yes' to activities that are important to you, or say 'no' to what you don't want to do. When you delete 'I should' from your vocabulary, and shift into the energy of 'I could...', 'I get to...', or 'I love to...', you will feel liberated – whatever you choose to do.

In the Nourishing Friendships Workbook, which accompanies this book, I take you through a 'should' exercise that helps you decide to do things or not – without feeling you 'should' or feeling guilty.

Letting go of any feelings of guilt

When you start saying 'no', you might feel guilty about doing so. Don't worry, it's normal to have doubts when developing new habits. It becomes easier in time. Check out Chapter 17 for tips on how to manage your emotions and let go of any negative feelings such as guilt. EFT (tapping) is a really effective way to do this and easy to learn.

Remember, you're not responsible for what other people do or how they feel, e.g. how they treat you, if they want a friendship when you don't, or whether they get upset when you say 'no' – either because they don't like rejection or perhaps they're not used to people saying 'no' to them.

All you can control is what you think, feel, do, and say, and the way you communicate your response. The most important thing is for you to do what it takes to get your own needs met, say 'no' kindly yet firmly, let go of any negative emotions you feel about doing this, and walk away with your head held high, knowing you've done the best you can.

Note: If you're in an unhealthy, abusive, or narcissistic relationship, make sure you have the support of others and are safe to stand up to the other person before saying 'no'.

Key points

- You can say 'no', and still be a nice, kind person.

- When you say 'no' to others, you're saying 'yes' to yourself. You deserve to get your own needs and desires met!

- You can't control how others respond when you say 'no'. Their needs, emotional triggers, and behaviours are not your responsibility. However, you are the only person who can speak your truth.

- You always have the right to say 'no' although it's still important to make sure you feel safe and don't put yourself in danger by saying 'no'. If this is a concern, get the support you need first.

- Continuing to say 'yes' when you'd like to say 'no' will keep you trapped.

- Saying 'no' when that is what you want, is a healthy friendship habit to nurture.

Activity: Be prepared. Make a list of all the situations you'd like to say 'no' to and draft wording for what you could say the next time they come up.

Chapter 21
Resolving Conflicts and Making Up With Friends

Navigating adversity can enrich your friendships

As we grow and have diverse life experiences, our views and opinions can differ from our closest friends, which can sometimes cause disagreements, upsets, or conflict. It's also human to make mistakes and unintentionally upset each other because of emotional triggers from the past, for either party.

Conflict resolution is one of the most valuable skills you can learn and apply in all walks of life. And while this is a complex topic, there are three simple steps you can use to make it easier to resolve issues and conflicts with friends, with a view to maintaining the friendship.

∿

I used to be someone who avoided conflict at all costs. I was scared that if I spoke up, I would lose a friendship, partner, or job. That was until I was discussing an underperforming member of my team with my manager at work. She told me, it was either me or the team member who was underperforming. She was right. It was my responsibility to resolve the situation. Almost thirty years later, I still remember that valuable life lesson: failure to deal with issues is a form of self-harming.

Avoiding conflict causes harm and distress

If you avoid conflict, ask yourself, what impact does this have on your happiness, health, and relationships?

Given how easy it is to misinterpret someone or unwittingly activate one of their emotional triggers, I wonder if too many friendships fall apart simply because people don't dare to speak up. When you don't deal with issues or differences of opinion, you can start to feel resentful, angry, stressed, or distance yourself from those involved. And these negative feelings can fester and intensify over time, eating away at what could otherwise could be a good relationship.

Dealing with issues

Good friends communicate openly to resolve issues with compassion, and doing this can often strengthen the bond. However, some people who lack the courage to have difficult conversations, or who have been hurt in the past, opt for a zero-tolerance approach, cutting ties with friends abruptly without discussion, causing further unnecessary upset. I prefer to think that we all do the best we can in any moment and to accept that we all sometimes make mistakes. When you do this, you can give people the benefit of the doubt and explore ways to resolve issues, with a view to strengthening the friendship. I'd hate to think I've given up a good friendship because of a misunderstanding that could easily have been resolved.

A difficult conversation doesn't have to be a conflict

I've yet to meet anyone who likes conflict. Many avoid it. And few embrace it as the opportunity it is – to discuss a situation fully, openly, and honestly, from both perspectives. Becoming comfortable having difficult conversations can help to defuse and resolve issues so you feel better again, irrespective of the outcome.

As long as you feel safe to have the conversation, discussing and tackling challenges straight away can often lead to better relationships. Sometimes, yes, you may fall out temporarily or a friendship might end. But it's better to lose a friendship knowing you've done your best rather than giving in to fears and anxieties, or be left wondering, what if? If need be, you could involve a third-party facilitator or coach to help you work out the best way forward.

We have a better and deeper friendship now

I was discussing this with a good friend recently, as we'd faced a challenging situation a few years ago. We're both proud of how we handled it and love how it has deepened our connection. I honestly don't know many other people I'd have been able to have this conversation with, let alone someone I'd only known a few years. We remain good friends, and I'm grateful to her for permitting me to share our story, from both our perspectives.

～

My perspective: We'd planned to go on holiday together until we disagreed about some aspects of the arrangements. This first became apparent via an email I received from her. We both quickly agreed it would be best to discuss it face-to-face.

Looking back on that initial conversation, we're both impressed by how we handled ourselves. At the outset, we agreed to be open and honest with each other and act from a place of love, kindness, and compassion. We also shared our desire to continue to be friends. Yes, during the conversation there were tears, but we listened to each other and unpacked what had happened. By the end, we both felt heard and respected. We both also accepted we'd each had a part to play in the misunderstanding.

It took another couple of conversations for us to discuss and agree on a way forward, but we did and now I'm so pleased to consider her a good friend who inspires me and enriches my life in so many ways. We have since had many great adventures together.

～

My friend's perspective: Alisoun and I enjoyed a really lovely friendship and something came up which jarred a little. I wondered about whether to raise it and realised that when you value a friendship and something jars within it, then you have a choice to make. If you choose to say nothing, then the issue will eat away at the roots of that friendship, and it will ultimately wither on the vine. If you choose to tackle the issue, then another decision arises: do you want to stay in the friendship and work at moving past the issue, or is the issue more important than the friendship?

I was very clear that I didn't want this friendship to wither on the vine. And that whilst the issue was important, I wanted us to work through it and to come out stronger on the other side.

I was relieved to find Alisoun wanted that, too. The very first thing that we spoke about before delving into the issue was the shared intention to remain as friends and, if possible, to build an even stronger friendship as a result of working through something which was undoubtedly going to be difficult for both of us.

And that is exactly what happened. I am delighted to say that our friendship is deeper and has, at least from my point of view, shifted from the 'friends vibe' to a 'sister vibe'; that feeling when you're in a family and the relationship can sustain both the smooth and the rough of life.

Focus on positive intentions and what you can control and influence

It takes both parties to agree they want to continue in a friendship for that to happen. However, that may not always be possible if the disagreement highlights a significant breach of trust, conflicting values, needs, or wants from the friendship. The self-esteem, mental and emotional well-being, and capacity of both parties to forgive each other are also huge influencing factors on whether the friendship can survive.

The point of conflict resolution conversations is to explore the potential for resolution while also being unattached to outcomes. By focusing on your positive intentions, actions, and coming from a place of love, kindness, and compassion, you're more likely to leave knowing that you've done your best, no matter what the outcome is. That is the best you can do.

Remember you can't control whether others will want to continue to be friends. If the other party is not interested in patching things up, it's then best to focus on what you can control and influence, e.g. processing any negative feelings you have, such as loss, grief, or anger, so you can move on.

How to resolve issues depends on the scope of the issue

Obviously, how to resolve any issue with friends depends on the type and scope of the issue concerned. These could include:

- You or a friend crossing a line due to you both having different values, boundaries or expectations.

- A misunderstanding – as each of you has had different life experiences, and mis-interpretations of communications happen to some extent most of the time.

- A heated discussion or argument where one (or both) of you was angry.

- A breach of trust – be mindful that we all have different ideas about what constitutes a breach of trust or unacceptable behaviours.

- You or the other person was mean, critical, or said something hurtful – either on a one-off or regular basis.

- You've fallen out with a friend.

- You feel you need to have a 'difficult' conversation with a friend to resolve something that's come up – like the example I shared earlier.

Three steps towards resolving issues with friends

Sometimes a simple apology is all you need to move past an issue that's arisen in a friendship. However, for more complex or serious issues, you may find this three-step process helpful in revolving issues and conflicts with friends: prepare, discuss, and reflect.

1. Prepare

Take time to prepare before all conversations:

- Consider how much you value the friendship and want to invest in resolving this.

- Get clarity on the real issue. Sometimes what's triggered an outburst or disagreement is the last straw or only part of a bigger issue to be addressed. It's easier to resolve conflict when you know what the real issue is. If you're unsure, this may need to be part of the initial conversation you have with your friend.

- Reflect on the part which you played in the situation. Sometimes it can be hard to admit, but you've had a part to play in the upset. See Chapter 7.

- Consider the situation from your perspective plus that of the other person, and of a detached observer. From each perspective, consider their desired outcome, how they could perceive things differently, what you agree on, what's important, plus potential objections and solutions.

- Draft what you need and want in advance, from a perspective that's most likely to be heard.

- Put yourself in a positive emotional state, e.g. one of love, kindness, or compassion, before communicating with the other party.

- If meeting up face-to-face, arrange a neutral venue.

2. Discuss

During the conversation:

- Agree on your desired outcomes at the start of the conversation, e.g. for both parties to feel heard and safe enough to speak honestly. To be treated with love, kindness, respect, and compassion.

- Start from points of agreement, e.g. that you don't want to hurt each other, or that you both want to stay friends.

- Apologise for the part you've played at the outset and, as appropriate, throughout the conversation.

- Give each other time to speak. Listen and don't interrupt the other person.

- Repeat back what you understand they are saying to minimise further misinterpretations.

- Identify and discuss the main issue(s) and potential solutions.

- Make sure you say everything you want to say.

- Agree on a way forward. Sometimes you'll be able to resolve a situation in one conversation but it may take more. Or you may find you can't agree on a way forward other than to agree to disagree and let the friendship go.

3. Reflect

Conflict resolution is an opportunity to learn and grow, whatever the outcome. To do this, reflect on what went well, what you've learned, and what you'd do differently in the future. It's also worth considering what you need to forgive yourself and the other person for, as well as taking action to let go of any emotional distress this has caused. See Chapter 17 on Managing Your Emotions.

You can use this process to help resolve all kinds of issues. In the example I shared earlier about an issue I had with my friend, we hadn't had an argument or fallen out. It was simply a difference of opinion on something important that we needed to discuss. However, I still followed this process, and thankfully we're now closer than ever.

Making up with friends

Where you've fallen out with a friend, the above process will help you to put the situation into perspective and to discuss the best way forward, for both you and your friend.

Before trying to make up, it's also important to consider what you love about the friendship and whether what happened was a one-off issue, or just one of many red flags. In the next chapter I share factors to consider before ending a friendship, which you might also find helpful in deciding whether to make up with a friend.

Where it's been a small, isolated issue, picking up the friendship again might simply involve apologies and continuing as you were before. However, for more complex issues, it might be a good time to re-set the friendship, e.g. by sharing what you love about your friend, clarifying boundaries, and discussing aspirations you both have for the friendship.

Apologising to friends

Whether you've had a big argument, fallen out, or unintentionally upset someone, the authenticity and scope of your apology is critical. The preparation stage of the above process can help you work out what to do, if the situation needs more than simply saying 'sorry'.

What to say and how best to apologise will depend on the issue and type of friendship you have. Here are some ideas:

- Say you're sorry, in a way that conveys you mean it.

- Tell them what specifically you're sorry for – I once remember someone apologising for 'what happened yesterday', yet to me there had been several things they'd said that had upset me. By simply saying you're sorry, the other person may not be clear what you're sorry for.

- Tell them how much you love, appreciate them, and value their friendship (as long as you do).

- Choose how you want to communicate your apology – a phone call, meeting up, letter, or text. Be mindful, it's often easier for written communications to be mis-interpreted, because when you're not present, it can be harder to gauge their response and correct any further misunderstandings that arise. I personally find it best to talk to people unless they are reluctant to do this, or they've been challenging in the past and I know their reactions would put me off communicating my intended message.

Remember, you can't always keep others happy, and as part of moving forward friends may want you to compromise your needs or values so they can be happy. But if you were to do that, you'd not have a healthy friendship. Focus on apologising for the part you played in the situation, while also communicating your needs and boundaries, as appropriate.

Key points

- Conflicts with friends are natural and, if handled well, can deepen and enrich a relationship. If you feel uncomfortable doing this, you're not alone. But you can become better at apologising and having challenging conversations.

- Failure to resolve issues can make a situation worse and potentially unnecessarily cost you a friendship.

- Knowing you've done the best you can feels good – whatever the outcome of your conversations.

Activity: Think of a past issue with a friend. Consider the part you played and reflect on what you'd do differently.

Chapter 22
Ending Friendships

As one friendship ends, space is created for a better one

∾

A young woman inspired me to write this chapter. While still at high school, she realised she no longer liked her bitchy, mean friends. So she decided to completely change her friendship group. There were no big fallouts or dramas. She simply stopped hanging out with them after one particular night out. Instead, she started spending more time with kinder, more positive people. In doing so, she went from being desperate to leave school to deciding to stay on until the end of her final year. I am in awe of her courage. I know I wouldn't have been brave enough to do that at her age.

∾

I'm sure you'll have had many friendships end, as we all do. Most are likely to have faded away quietly without any conflict or fallout. You simply drifted apart. However, you may also have had friendships that broke down more memorably.

Of my survey respondents, 39% – representing 4 in 10 midlife women – wanted to know how to end a friendship with love and compassion.

The focus on this chapter is how to end a friendship so that you find it easier to do this in the future. However, I want to encourage you to first evaluate whether ending the friendship is the only and best way forward.

Factors to consider before ending a friendship

Whatever the reason for a friendship deteriorating, it's always worth considering the following before ending the relationship:

- **What's changed or gone wrong?** – take time to reflect on not only what's just happened, but also events that have led up to this over the last few months.

- **The part you've played** – it may be hard to admit but there's likely to be a part you've played, even if that's only been choosing to be in the friendship. Could you have said something better? How could you have reacted better?

- **The part your friend plays in your life** – cutting off a friend isn't always the best way forward. If you think about the time and effort put into making relationships work with life partners, why would you not do the same with long-term friends? First, consider the balance of ways in which they enrich your life versus their negative behaviours and the impact ending the friendship would have on you and other relationships. Then, if you feel the emotional turmoil outweighs the benefits of staying friends, it may be time to take a break or end the friendship – even if it breaks your heart.

- **The potential for reconciliation** – depending on the situation, it may be worth considering whether a discussion to resolve the issue is worth exploring. It would be such a shame to end a friendship based on a misunderstanding, or an unusual negative behaviour or reaction, especially for friends with whom you've had a good long-term relationship. See the previous chapter for tips on resolving conflicts with friends.

- **How long you've been friends** – building friendships takes time and effort. It's easier to let go of friendships at the early stages by simply pulling back and being less proactive, while still being kind and polite. However, if you've been friends with someone for years, there are a lot more things to consider, including the most respectful way to communicate why you need to end the friendship.

'Learn to let go of the so-called friends. They are not worth it. You are worth more. Value the true friends who care about you and want to connect with you. It's hard to let go but if the friendship doesn't bring you joy, it is not a true friendship. Yes, this can feel like a divorce or bereavement, but it will pass and you will be free and uncluttered to form new friendships.' Catherine

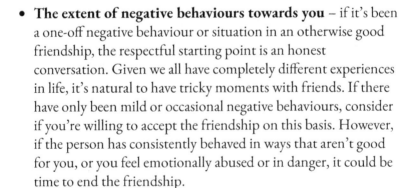

- **The extent of negative behaviours towards you** – if it's been a one-off negative behaviour or situation in an otherwise good friendship, the respectful starting point is an honest conversation. Given we all have completely different experiences in life, it's natural to have tricky moments with friends. If there have only been mild or occasional negative behaviours, consider if you're willing to accept the friendship on this basis. However, if the person has consistently behaved in ways that aren't good for you, or you feel emotionally abused or in danger, it could be time to end the friendship.

- **Other support you have** – as with ending a romantic relationship, you may still love and appreciate your friend when you decide it's best to end the friendship. Sometimes you can feel torn between wanting to stay friends yet knowing you need to let the friendship go. That is natural. As is grieving for the loss of the relationship. That's where having a good support team around you can help you cope better. If the friend concerned is also an emotional crutch for you, it may be worth exploring how to put alternative support in place before ending the friendship. In the absence of other friends, consider speaking to a counsellor, therapist, or life coach, who can help you with this and work out the best way forward.

Alternatives to ending a friendship

Sometimes breaking all contact with a friend may feel too much and be unnecessary. Here are a couple of alternatives:

- **Take a break** – in a similar way that some romantic partnerships benefit from time apart, you can do the same with friendships. Time and space can give invaluable insights about the best way forward for your relationship. This may be a need you have and a boundary you communicate to your friend. Or this may be something you both discuss and agree on. Sometimes you may feel ready to put a timeframe on this. In other situations you may feel you need to see how things go first.

- **Accept the friendship has changed** – just because you've had a close friendship with someone in the past doesn't mean it has to stay that way. The nature of friendships can change over time, e.g. a close friend may become someone you now only see occasionally for nostalgic reasons, or you may decide to only see people in a group rather than on a one-to-one basis.

Reasons friendships end

Friendships end for a number of reasons including: you've made poor friendship choices in the past; you've allowed people to mistreat you; you've mistreated others, shown a lack of care or support, or haven't invested in the friendship; one of you has become more self-assured or confident and has outgrown the other person; your lives are going off in different directions; one of you has activated an emotional trigger in the other person, such as jealousy, fear of rejection, or anger; one of you has breached the trust of the other person; there's been a disagreement, misunderstanding, or poor communication; you have a clash of values, personality, or behaviours, or an opposing point of view that's too big to move past.

How to end friendships

Once you've considered the above factors, if you still want to end a friendship, there are two 'kind' ways to do this: either let the friendship drift apart naturally, as most relationships do over time; or tell the person concerned you no longer want to be friends with them.

How you physically end a friendship depends on how you would usually communicate with that friend, what you find easier, and the best way to get your message across. It's also important to communicate this in a way that's the right balance of being firm and respectful while also being aligned with your values, e.g. honesty, integrity, kindness, and compassion.

- **Tell your friend why you no longer want to be friends** – without a doubt it takes courage to do this, but for close friends, having a conversation with them is the most respectful thing to do. Especially if you were close friends or would usually chat, see each other, or send each other gifts/cards.

- **Let the friendship fade away** – if you feel there is nothing left that needs to be said, do nothing and let the friendship drift apart naturally. This is what happens in many friendships. It's often easier to do this with newer or more distant acquaintances than people you've known for a long time. Obviously, if the other person attempts to keep the friendship going, it's only courteous and respectful to let them know why you no longer want to be friends.

- **Avoid ghosting** – I believe ghosting (ending a friendship suddenly without explaining why) is the coward's way out. It is rude, disrespectful, cruel, and hurtful.

Whatever form you choose (e.g. in person, via a phone call, email or letter), carefully plan what you're going to say first, and rehearse or edit it several times beforehand.

What to say to end a friendship

As with all aspects of friendship, it's for you to decide the best style and words to use that feel authentic to you.

My style is to start with what I think is the most compassionate way to deliver this kind of message, using the UHT model (see Chapter 18) to explain why you no longer want to be friends. In this situation, you could replace the first part with how much you've enjoyed, valued, or appreciated their friendship. Sometimes, however, you need to be more direct to get your message across.

Bear in mind that one-way communications such as text messages, emails, or letters, can leave more scope for misunderstanding. However, here are some examples of what you could say to end a friendship:

- We have a very different approach to life, so I don't think we're a good fit for each other.

- You've breached my trust. I no longer want to be friends.

- You never stand up for me and regularly put me down. I don't want to be around you anymore.

- I'm not willing to compromise my values or ethics, simply because you don't agree with me or don't like what I'm doing. If that's what you expect me to do, this friendship is over.

- I find it hard to cope with your constant negativity and criticism so don't want to continue to see you.

- While we have a lot in common, we seem to wind each other up. So, let's agree to be civil to each other at group events and accept that we don't need to be close friends.

- I hear you're having a hard time, and I want to support you. But it's not OK for you to keep sending me abusive messages. So let's take a break from each other.

- Don't contact me again. I don't want to be friends with you anymore.

- I don't like the way you treat me, so stay away from me.

Remember, you can't control how someone will react. Occasionally, people may agree or be relieved, although some could be upset or angry. All you can do is focus on doing whatever it takes for you to walk away from the conversation and friendship knowing that you did your best.

How to cope when a friendship ends

Irrespective of who ends the friendship, you may feel a level of loss, grief, or sadness – especially for formerly close long-term friendships. Or you may experience relief, anger, rejection, shock, or devastation.

~

I once had a good friend return a gift to me. There was no message saying why but making it clear she'd closed the door to reconciliation. I was devastated at the time and it took years to get over. To this day, I don't know what I did to upset her but I respected her decision and realised I'd misjudged how much (or in reality, how little) she valued our friendship.

~

However you feel, there are several ways to navigate your way through what can be an emotionally challenging time:

- **Accept the part you played** – even if you feel you've done nothing wrong, you will have had a part to play in the friendship breakdown, e.g. you chose to be friends, you allowed the other person to mistreat you for too long, you spoke your truth, you ended the friendship, stood up for yourself, reacted in a way you don't feel proud of, or acted with love and compassion. If you've chosen to end an abusive or unhealthy relationship, remember to congratulate yourself, too.

- **Focus on what you can control** – the only things you have scope to control are your own thoughts, feelings, actions, and behaviours, as I discussed in Chapters 7, 10, and 17. For example, you could see this as an opportunity to make new friends who share a similar interest or passion. Or to spend more time with people you've met in the past that you'd like to get to know better.

- **Manage your emotions naturally** – it hurts to lose friends, particularly those you have been close to. That's where techniques such as EFT (tapping) can be really helpful in helping you to let go of negative emotions such as guilt, regret, sadness, or loss. This includes forgiving yourself and the other person. Forgiveness isn't about agreeing with others' actions. Rather, it's one of the most powerful ways to release yourself from upset. As long as you hold onto negative emotions towards others, you give your power away to them. Instead, choose to be kind to yourself and do what it takes to heal from your loss in ways that are healthy. See Chapter 17.

- **Get support** – find people you can speak to about how you feel, ideally people who are not connected to the other person, e.g. another friend, family, a counsellor, life coach, or therapist.

- **Spend time with nourishing friends** – replace your old friendships with new, life-enriching ones. It may take time to build new friendships but it will be worth it. Enjoy the process.

Key points

- Many friendships fade away naturally if you don't put time and effort into maintaining them. Most friends are only in your life temporarily.

- Before deciding whether to proactively end a friendship, explore whether there are are other options that would be a better way forward for you.

- When communicating you want to end a friendship, do this in a way that aligns with your values, e.g. love, kindness, compassion, and respect.

- You can't control how others react. Instead, focus on doing whatever it takes for you to feel you've done the right thing.

- If you're upset about a friendship ending, explore how to heal your grief and feel better again.

- It's only through letting go of friendships that no longer serve you that you have space for new ones to grow. Remember, your life reflects the friends you surround yourself with. So, choose who you spend time with wisely.

You've got this! Remember, you deserve to be treated well, and it's better to let a challenging unhealthy friendship go. In doing so, you'll free up more time to spend with new nourishing friends.

Chapter 23
Rekindling Friendships

People who are meant to be in your life will always gravitate back towards you

Have you ever thought about a good friend from the past and wondered if it would be a good idea to get back in touch with them? Rekindling a friendship could be one of the easiest ways to develop a deep connection with someone again – particularly if you simply drifted apart.

∾

'My mother used to say, "Make new friends but keep the old. One is silver, the other is gold." You learn the wisdom of that later in life. Old friends can come back into your life after years apart, and you can take up exactly where you left off. These friends are gold. You know they care about you, want the best for you, and have always wanted the best for you even when they have not been physically around.' Catherine

∾

In this chapter, you'll find tips for rekindling friendships so you find it easier to revive relationships with people you'd like in your life again.

Ten tips for rekindling past friendships

As I've said throughout this book, it's natural for friendships to come and go as we all dance through life to slightly different beats. The people worth reconnecting with are usually those you really like and enjoy being around – either friends you've lost touch with or acquaintances you wish you'd got to know better. It doesn't matter, as long as they make you feel good. Here are ten tips for rekindling friendships:

1. Remember why the friendship ended

Consider why the friendship ended before deciding to rekindle it. If you simply drifted apart because of busy lives, changing priorities, or either of you moved away, there may be scope to revive your friendship. However, rekindling the friendships that ended because of arguments, fights, or unhealthy behaviours, may not be wise.

2. Get clear on the type of friends you want in your life

This relates to what we covered in Chapters 9 and 12. You may not know the other person's current situation or interests, but if you got on well and had a similar approach to life or shared values or interests, there's the possibility they could be good friends again.

3. Keep your approach positive and light-hearted

The purpose of reaching out initially is simply to say hello and see whether they are interested in reconnecting. Whether by letter, text, or phone call, keep your message short, light-hearted, and positive. Let them know you are thinking about them, and ask if they want to catch up. It's natural to feel vulnerable doing this, so take small steps. You could suggest a call, cuppa, or walk.

4. Treat the friendship as a new one

Reconnecting with old friends is an opportunity to get to know each other again and determine whether you're a good fit for one another at this stage of life. It's not about trying to make an old friendship work, but about exploring whether people from the past have a place in the future you want for yourself. Accept the form of your friendship could be different to what you enjoyed in the past.

5. Let go of any expectations

Expectations can often lead to disappointments. It's healthier to embrace a hopeful mindset that allows for the potential you will rekindle a friendship while remaining unattached to any outcomes. Be open to the possibility they may want to explore being friends again. If they say 'yes' that's great. If not, move on to the next person.

6. Be mindful that your friend may have changed

You're both likely to have changed since you last saw each other. This isn't always a bad thing. New interests and perspectives often enhance friendships, as long as you both still have a good connection.

7. Accept the person they are now

In the same way that I assume you want to be accepted and liked for being the person you are now, whoever they show up as is fine, too. You may discover you easily pick up where you left off and want to be in each other's lives again. Or you may find the conversation is stilted, you've nothing in common, or you don't want to spend more time with them. Acknowledge the truth of the situation without judgment.

8. Let the friendship go if there is no connection

If you discover you're no longer a good fit, that's OK. Good friendships need mutual desire to continue. If either of you decides 'no', it doesn't make either of you a bad person; you've simply moved on. Crossing them off your list of potential friends creates space for the right people. It's obviously easier to do this if the other person doesn't appear eager to meet up again. However, it may be worth preparing something to say in advance, just in case they want to rekindle the friendship but you don't, e.g. using the UHT model from Chapter 20.

9. Respect if people say 'no' or don't get back to you

It can feel vulnerable putting yourself out there and reaching out to people. But if you don't do this, you'll never know. And at least this way you won't regret not asking. Remember, though, when someone says 'no' or doesn't get back to you, it's not always about you. If you find this hard, check out Chapter 17 to learn how to manage your emotions so you find it easier to let go and move on to the next person.

10. Nurture the friendships you want in your life

When you both feel the connection is still there, celebrate together and nurture the relationship to become close friends again. See Chapter 15 for tips on how to do this.

Key points

- If you had a good connection with a friend in the past, they may make a good friend for you again.

- Before reaching out to rekindle a friendship, remind yourself why you're not currently friends and consider if the person could be the kind of friend you want in the future.

Activity: If you have any friendships you'd like to consider rekindling, what insights are you taking away from this chapter?

Chapter 24
Wisdom From Women Over 60

Valuable insights that only come from experience

Recognising I'm only fifty-six, I asked women over sixty to share their friendship wisdom. Some of their insights are scattered throughout this book. Here I share their consolidated tips for younger women, their experience of friendships at their age, and tips for retirement.

What tips would you give your younger yourself?

- Friendship is a gift freely given. Good friends are like family and will be there for you through the good and tough times, if you're nice to them. More time spent on friends seems to come back your way in kindness.

- It's never too late to make new friends. Be open to surprises and new friends as well as treasuring the old. Don't put all your eggs in one basket.

- Choose your friends carefully – quality people who share your values, interests, and approach to life. Friends help you, sometimes more than family, so tend close friendships with love and always ensure you put yourself on equal footing with mutual respect.

- Cultivate friendships with people of all ages. When you get older, people often need help in various areas and younger friends may be able to help. It keeps you thinking young, too!

- Have a small circle of close friends or as many friends as possible – whatever feels right for you. I find it easier to support a few close friends but also need acquaintances, too.

- Treasure friendships with people you connect with the most; those you feel a special connection with who celebrate you as you celebrate them. Take your time with new friendships and let them develop naturally. Nurture and keep in touch with good friends all through life.

- Friends come and go. Tend your closest ones with love and nurture deep and meaningful relationships with them – despite the distance, partners, marriages, children, and comings and goings. Keep your door open. You never know how the friendship will unfold or when the time may be right for you to reconnect with someone. If it no longer fits, let it go. Same for friendships, husbands, and bras!

- Go with the ebbs and flows of long-term relationships. Friendships evolve and change as we go through life. A best friend can suddenly turn their back on you. Likewise, someone who was once a stranger or distant acquaintance could become a good friend.

- Talk things out with friends. Don't let difficult issues lead to breaches. Be kind. Hold space for your friends, don't judge them, and give advice if asked but don't expect them to take it. Love them now, yesterday, and tomorrow.

How would you describe your friendships now?

- My friendships now are far more fulfilling because I'm more selective about the friends I choose to spend time with. They are deeper, more authentic, and carefully nurtured. Warts and all, but less dramatic. I realise the value of true friends.

- Friendships weren't so important when I was younger. They are now. You'll lose some friends through natural wastage, so make time for good friends. You'll need them later in life.

- My long-term friends are so important to me – people who know my history or who met my parents. They help keep a link to my past and family. It's good to get back together even after a long absence.

- I find it easier to make new friends now as I'm not spending thirty-six hours at work and I'm doing more activities where I meet people. I have a wider variety of friends – some I've known for many years, but lots of new friends, too.

- It's much harder to make friends versus when I was in my twenties when I had close work friends. Now, people spend more time with families and grandchildren and have less time to be with friends. It's also harder to find places to meet new friends if you're not as active as you used to be, or you have relocated to somewhere new later in life.

- As a single woman over sixty, I find it difficult to find a partner but easy to find new friends. They fill part of the 'gap'. It seems so easy to communicate with women our age and find common ground, while it's harder with men.

- I'm more assertive in making sure I get my needs met in the friendships. I need a mixture of old and new friends with similar interests, beliefs, and morals, who treat me well.

- I'm more accepting of others, interested in differences, and less envious of others. I had expectations of my friends and judged a lot when I was younger. I go with the flow much more now, understand differing intentions more, and forgive people.

- As you get older, your friends can often be there for you more than family, especially if they live nearby. I believe that in dire circumstances your true friends shine through.

- I'm grateful for the friendships I had during my working life, and the multitude of friends in my life now, created at every stage of my journey – some fleeting and others for life.

∾

'I welcome women who refuse to bow down to societal norms. Ageing with audacity is my theme.' Michelle

∾

What impact did retirement have on your friendships?

- Lots of my friends are retired, too. We're free to do as we please and see each other more often, having fun days out. There is far more time to share fun and laughter – no 'school' nights to curtail enjoyment.

- Suddenly many friends I had through working together have become nothing more than ex-colleagues. True friends feel more vital to me in retirement. It's still early days but I'm exploring whether I still have anything other than work in common with some people I worked with.

- Initially there were fewer opportunities for daily socialising and contact with people, with work out of the picture. Some of my friends still worked and were unavailable during the day. I've had to make more of an effort to socialise, meet up, and stay in touch with people. As friends retire, you have more time to reconnect with the true friends.

- I miss my day-to-day friendships with younger folk. I have to go out of my way to meet people who are not in a similar demographic group.

- A bonus for me has been getting a free bus pass because of my age. I arrange to see friends from further afield, regularly visiting interesting destinations and events together around the country. On a local level, I've more time to meet friends for lunch, walks, curry nights, and going to shows.

- Since finishing work I've taken up new hobbies. I've joined a sea swimming group and formed wonderful and deep new friendships.

- Being self-employed meant I didn't leave work but simply reduced my hours when I got my pension. There's been little impact on my friendships in retirement other than that I have more time to see them while working when I feel like it.

- There's more space in retirement for friends, new interests, and spiritual connections as life moves forward.

- For me, not being in the workplace has improved my friendship base. Working took so much of my time and energy. It was hard work for me. Now I'm free and have time to spend at leisure with friends and explore meeting all sorts of people.

- My friendships in retirement are much better! You have more time to catch up with friends that work, or children didn't allow time for, or because of distances. I've been so delighted to meet up with friends from over thirty years ago for holidays rather than just a quick meal. It's like the last thirty years slipped away, and we are young again with such laughter and joy. We're definitely growing old disgracefully!

- Friendships are great in retirement, a bit like my student days. I see old friends more often, as we are all retired and are free to do as we please. I have always found it easy to have good friendships by being honest, kind, compassionate, caring, and interested in the other person and the details of their lives.

Conclusion

As with all other stages of life, the same message shines through: friendships in your wisdom years depend upon your life experience, mindset, skills, and how you select and choose to engage with friends.

I feel we need another word for retirement, and it's reassuring that those I surveyed are clearly challenging the outdated concept of retiring from life too.

To me it's about embracing this season of life with love, gratitude, curiosity, and adventure. I call it 'adventurement'.

Here's to you having many joyful adventures with friends for years to come!

Chapter 25
What You Do Next Matters!

Every moment is a choice point

A growing swell of people are ripping up outdated beliefs about midlife, ageing, and retirement. Instead, they are choosing to embrace ageing as a privilege, making the most of life, and having fun for as much of their time on this planet as possible. This means there are endless possibilities for you to make friends who will enrich your life for years to come – as soon as you choose to make this happen.

My grandad's favourite animal was an elephant. I remember one morning he drew three elephants on a blackboard on their kitchen wall. As children, we loved them, which is no doubt why they survived on that blackboard for years.

But how about the elephant who stomps around your mind when you think about making friends? I wonder if she ever says,

- I can't...
- I'm too old...
- I'm not good enough...
- I'm scared...
- I don't want to make a fool of myself...

- I can't be bothered...
- What happens if...?

Your inner elephant will try to talk you out of almost anything – tempting you to give in to doubts, fears, worries, anxieties, or emotional triggers created when you were younger. Yet when you do this, you may be doing yourself out of wonderful experiences and friendships, and a happier, healthier, more meaningful life.

So, can you retrain your inner elephant? Your gorgeous, dependable, loyal friend, who only wants what's best for you?

Here's the thing: elephants are one of the most intelligent creatures on the planet and learn new tricks easily. In fact, while elephants have incredible memories and like their well-worn routes, they're also curious animals.

~

I used to have doubts that meant I'd hold myself back from trying out new things and doing things by myself. They also caused me to stay in relationships with people who mistreated me for too long. But through being curious, reading, and attending personal development courses, I learned to be more confident and get to know and like the authentic woman I've become. I'm much better at selecting and maintaining good friendships and standing up for myself.

If I hadn't had those mindset shifts and put into practice what I'd learned, I wouldn't be surrounded by nourishing friends. Nor would I be enjoying the wonderful, diverse life I have now.

~

Choosing to surround yourself with nourishing friends often requires a mindset shift and the mastery of new skills.

So tell me, what would you love to be different or better in your life? What difference would more nourishing friends make? What words of encouragement is your inner elephant whispering in your ear?

Your future happiness, and the friends you have around you, all depend on what you do next. Every choice you make will take you nearer or further away from the life and friendships you yearn for.

When you listen to your inner wisdom and embrace what's in this book, you'll be more likely to enjoy the future and friends you want. However, continuing to approach friendship as you've done in the past would mean you've wasted your time reading this book.

I invite you to take inspired action, focus on nourishing friendships, and bring all your ideas to life – so that you have plenty of like-minded friends to talk to and have fun with for years to come.

Remember, you are not alone. Many people wish they had more friends they could relate to and could enjoy life with. By inviting out people you connect with, you open the door to friendship for yourself and for others.

You've got this. You deserve to be happy and surrounded by nourishing friends.

What's the first thing you're going to do to make more friends?

Please Review on Amazon

Thanks for reading this book. If you've found it helpful, please take a moment to leave a five-star rating or review on Amazon.

It would mean a lot to me, and will help more people like you hear about this book, so they find it easier to enjoy good friendships too.

Use this QR code to review this book

More Nourishing Friendship Resources

Nourishing Friendship Workbook

Use this accompanying workbook – a mix of practical exercises and blank journal pages – to capture your thoughts and ideas from this book, so you find it easier to enjoy more good friendships. Check it out on Amazon or via my website – www.alisoun.com/books

Nourishing Friends Notebook

Use this to keep on top of new friendships and remember important information about your friends. Available on Amazon or via my website – www.alisoun.com/books

Other Nourishing Friendship Support & Resources

You don't need to do this alone. Check out group and one-to-one support so you find it easier to make friends and cope better with friendship challenges.

I also share more tips, blogs, videos, and other recommended resources on friendship on my website – alisoun.com/friends

Use this QR code to check out Alisoun's friendship resources

An Invitation to Connect

It would be fabulous to connect on social media too. See how to contact me via the links below.

Alisoun x

QR code for my website: alisoun.com/friends

facebook.com/alisounmac

instagram.com/alisounmac

youtube.com/alisounmac

Thank you

A huge thanks to both my parents for all the love, support, and inspiration for this book.

I'm also grateful to everyone who has been part of my friendship journey and the publication of this book. This includes all the fabulous nourishing friends I have in my life, those who were friends for a season, friends who have mistreated me, and friends I may have unintentionally hurt in the past. You've all contributed to how I approach friendships now and the insights I've shared in this book.

I'd also like to thank everyone who has contributed to the content of this book, attended my friendship events and courses, the women who completed my online survey, plus those who shared friendship experiences with me informally. You all gave me a broader perspective on friendship challenges that many women face.

With love and gratitude,

Alisoun x

About the author

Alisoun inspires and empowers women in their midlife years and beyond to live their best life and make a difference in the world. Her desire to help others make the most of life was first lit when she launched an independent travel club in 1994. She left a successful career in the investment industry to set up a coaching and wellbeing business in 2003. Since then Alisoun's talks, training, coaching, mentoring, online courses, books, podcasts, and humanitarian ventures have favourably changed the lives of thousands of people worldwide. She loves travelling and enjoying life by the sea in southeast Scotland. Find out more at alisoun.com

 facebook.com/alisounmac

 instagram.com/alisounmac

 youtube.com/alisounmac

Also by Alisoun Mackenzie

Books, Courses, and Journals

Heartatude, The 9 Principles of Heart-Centered Success

Want to change anything in your life or cope better with life's challenges? This book will show you how to make it happen.

Give-to-Profit How to Grow Your Business by Supporting Charities

Want to do good through your business? Read this book to discover the many ways to make a difference and optimise your impact.

My Meaningful Life Online Course

For women who want to create a joyful, meaningful life that lights up their heart and leaves a legacy they're proud of.

Adventure Journal for Women

If you love travel or adventures, this flexible adventure travel journal is for you. Enjoy more mini-adventures and breaks, and capture your memories.

Gratitude Journal

Reflect on the good things in life every day for 90 days so you feel better, cope better, and embrace life more.

Find out more at alisoun.com/shop

QR Code to alisoun.com/shop

Work With Alisoun

Alisoun works with midlife and retired women globally

Life Coaching and Feel-Good Sessions

One-to-one support to help you feel good, make friends, or embrace a new adventure – so you find it easier to make the most of life.

My Meaningful Life Coaching Programme

A one-to-one support programme for women who want to create a joyful meaningful life that lights up their heart and leaves a legacy they are proud of.

Business Mentoring

For heart-centered business owners wanting to set up or grow a business (full-time or part-time) so they can turn their passions into profits and make a difference in the world.

Invite Alisoun to Speak

Looking for an inspiring speaker for your conference, event, or podcast? Alisoun has been a popular motivational speaker for over twenty years and welcomes invitations to speak online or in person.

Find out more at alisoun.com

QR code for alisoun.com

We Call Them Friends

A poem by one of my friends, Ali Blevins

~

We call them friends but they are so much more; they are
    welcoming arms, an open door.

They are the voice of reason, a secret to tell, a shoulder to cry
    on, a bottomless well.

They are fun; they are laughter, frustration too, but never
    indifference; that would not do.

They have your back but will tell you straight, if you're being
    foolish or being great.

They will be there for you when times get rough and won't
    give up when the going's tough.

We call them friends, but they are so much more; they are
    sisters in life; our open door.

~

Check out more poems and art – aliblevinsart.com

Printed in Great Britain
by Amazon